IMAGES
of America

BUFFALO'S
PAN-AMERICAN EXPOSITION

IMAGES
of America

BUFFALO'S
PAN-AMERICAN EXPOSITION

Thomas E. Leary and Elizabeth C. Sholes

ARCADIA
PUBLISHING

Published by Arcadia Publishing
Charleston, South Carolina

Library of Congress Catalog Card Number: 2008923472

For all general information contact Arcadia Publishing at:
Telephone 843-853-2070
Fax 843-853-0044
E-mail sales@arcadiapublishing.com
For customer service and orders:
Toll-Free 1-888-313-2665

Visit us on the Internet at www.arcadiapublishing.com

CONTENTS

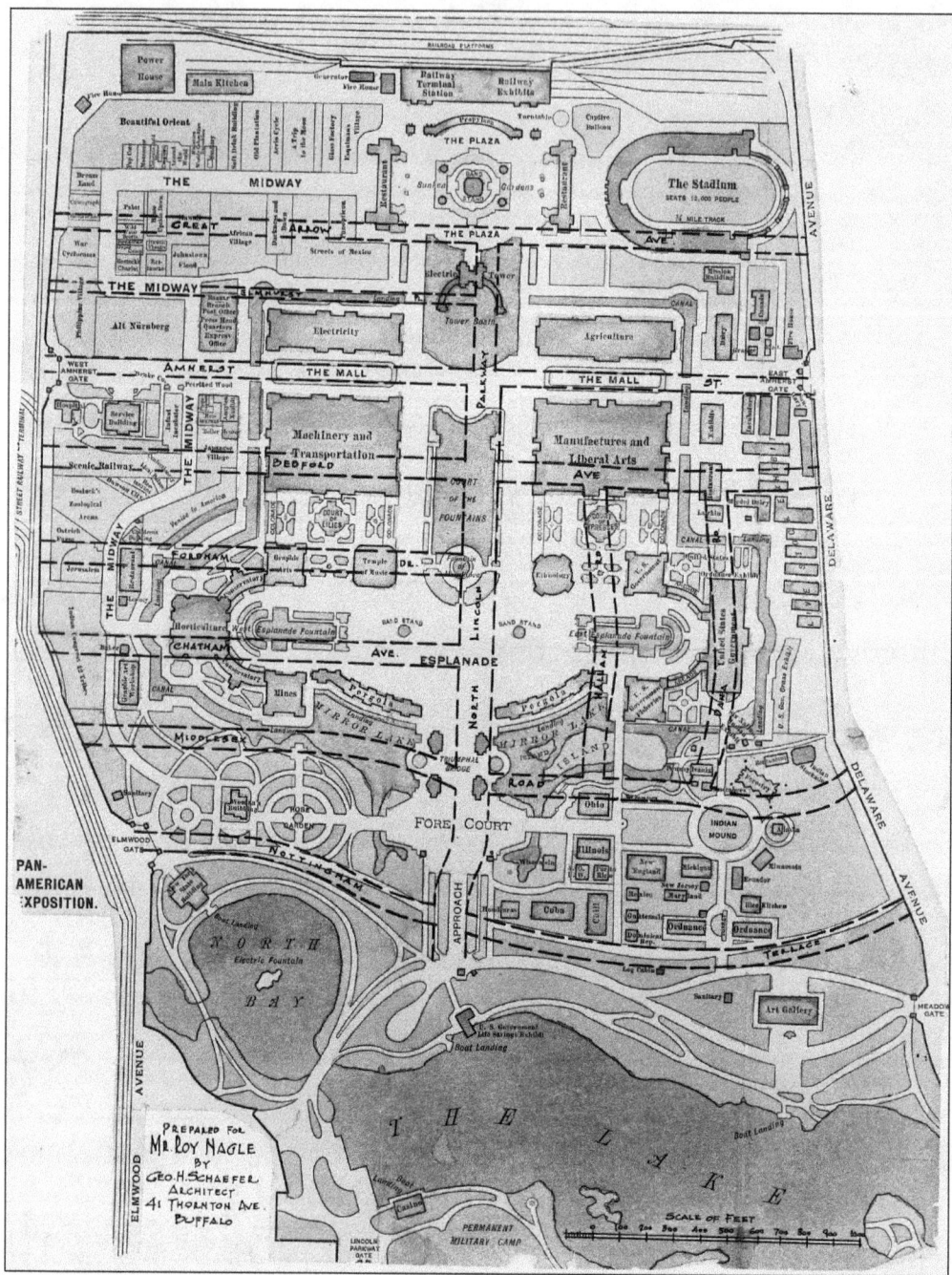

PAN-
AMERICAN
EXPOSITION.

Power House · Main Kitchen · Generator · Railway Terminal Station · Railway Exhibits · RAILROAD PLATFORMS

Beautiful Orient

THE PLAZA

The Stadium
SEATS 12,000 PEOPLE
¼ MILE TRACK

THE MIDWAY · GREAT · ARROW · THE PLAZA

THE MIDWAY · Alt Nürnberg · Electric Tower · Tower Basin

Electricity · Agriculture

AMHERST · THE MALL · THE MALL · ST.

WEST AMHERST GATE · EAST AMHERST GATE

Machinery and Transportation
BEDFORD AVE.

Manufactures and Liberal Arts
AVE.

COURT OF THE FOUNTAINS

THE MIDWAY · FORDHAM

Horticulture · West Esplanade Fountain · East Esplanade Fountain

CHATHAM · ESPLANADE

BAND STAND · SAND STAND

Pergola · MIRROR LAKE · Pergola · MIRROR L.

MIDDLESEX · TRIUMPHAL BRIDGE

ROAD · Ohio · INDIAN MOUND

ELMWOOD GATE · ROSE GARDEN

FORE COURT · Illinois · New England · Michigan

NOTTINGHAM · Cuba · New Jersey · Maryland

NORTH BAY
Electric Fountain

APPROACH · Ordnance

ELMWOOD AVENUE

U. S. Government Life Saving Exhibit
Boat Landing

Art Gallery · MEADOW GATE

DELAWARE AVENUE

TERRACE

THE LAKE

Boat Landing

PREPARED FOR
Mr. ROY NAGLE
BY
GEO. H. SCHAEFER
ARCHITECT
41 THORNTON AVE.
BUFFALO

SCALE OF FEET

LINCOLN PARKWAY GATE

PERMANENT MILITARY CAMP

INTRODUCTION

In the history of Buffalo, the Pan-American Exposition is both a moment and a memory. Between May and early November 1901, over 8 million people flocked to a temporary wonderland on a 350-acre site. They were dazzled by an array of monumental buildings housing hundreds of exhibits displaying the greatest material, scientific, and technological achievements of their time and place. If overwhelmed by this array, they could take refuge on the Midway with its funhouses, its amusements, and exotic curiosities. At night, the weary visitor could enjoy an electrical spectacle. *Harper's Weekly* said the best part of the Pan-Am was the summer night sky, the people, the beauty of the illuminated lagoons, and the electric lights everywhere.

The fair at Buffalo was part of a series of international expositions that had become increasingly more elaborate during the last half of the nineteenth century. The 1851 Crystal Palace Exposition in London is generally considered the prototype for this novel cultural institution. Other nations were inspired to copy and surpass the original. France conducted a series of memorable universal expositions in 1855, 1867, 1878, 1889, and 1900. Americans mimicked these European precedents and added their own novel features. Cities competed to host expositions to boost their economic fortunes and compensate for a sense of cultural inferiority compared to the capitals of Europe. Philadelphia staged a major exposition in 1876, as did Chicago in 1893. The promoters and planners in Buffalo also paid attention to the fairs held at Atlanta, Nashville, and Omaha during the late 1890s.

Within the half-century between the initial London venture and the Pan-Am, expositions expanded in scope and scale. They became manifestations of the industrial revolution and the global collisions between western civilization and other cultures. Initially, expositions focused on displays of technological innovation and product design. Commercialized entertainment was eventually added to education as an essential part of the fair's economic rationale.

The decision to have the 1901 international exposition in Buffalo had many roots. *Harper's Weekly* said it was because 1901 was the centennial of the first sale of building lots by Joseph Ellicott, agent for the Holland Land Company. The *Journal of American Industries* opined it was because Buffalo had "a delightful climate. . . on account of the breezes from Lake Erie" and that the city was exceptionally healthful "due somewhat to the fact that it has more asphalt pavements than any other city in the world" and "an abundance of pure water from Lake Erie and an extensive and perfect drainage system with proper sanitary regulations well-enforced."

An important component to the site selection was the desire of the Niagara Frontier to show off its achievements in massive hydroelectric generation and long-distance transmission.

Why a Pan-American theme? The events of the 1898 Spanish-American War played a major role. The U.S. defeat of a Spanish presence in the western hemisphere, as well as areas of the Pacific such as the Philippines, opened the doors to a new era of exploitation of Central and South America and the Caribbean. Thus Exposition planners vowed that no nations outside the Western Hemisphere would have a presence within the formal exhibits. They reinforced the thematic decision with the architectural motif; Spanish Renaissance design was selected as the unifying visual presentation of the ideal. Wherever possible, in exhibits or on the Midway, the Pan-American Exposition made clear that the United States was now the hemispheric if not the world's imperialist leader. "[I]t many fitly be called," said writer Herbert Croly, "not Pan-Americanism but Tinpan-Americanism."

But for the ordinary Buffalonian, it was an amazing spectacle. In the middle of a field north of the Scajaquada Creek, a city as breathtaking to turn-of-the-century Buffalo as Oz was to Dorothy rose suddenly, perfectly, dazzlingly, turning utilitarian farmland into a glittering wonder. It was accessible to all for only 25¢, a reasonable entry fee even in those days. People did come from near and far to witness this spectacle—their chance to see wonderful things and to experience a perfect, sanitized fantasy.

We have selected the images in this book from a variety of sources. Many represent the work of the Pan-Am's official photographer, Charles Dudley Arnold. A native of Canada, Arnold had come to Buffalo as a young man. His interest in photography developed during a stint as a traveling salesman after the Civil War. Early in his career, Arnold established a reputation as an architectural photographer. He toured Europe by dogcart ". . . to secure for American institutions and private subscribers a series of views of the best existing remains of classic architecture." As a supplier of images to leading architects, he had a leg up in winning the position as official photographer for the 1893 Chicago world's fair, a bastion of neo-classicism. Arnold reprised this role eight years later at the Pan-Am, exhaustively documenting its construction and physical setting as well as poking his lens into less formal nooks and crannies. He would photograph one more major exposition during his lifetime, the 1907 tercentenary of the founding of Jamestown, Virginia. Arnold died in Buffalo at the age of 83 in 1927.

To convey a sense of the exhibits inside as well as the sheer variety of everyday happenings around the grounds, we have included other images by professional and amateur photographers, supplemented by illustrations from newspapers, magazines, and trade journals. In addition, we have quoted extensively from journalists' comments about the Pan-Am and have introduced accounts left by ordinary visitors so that people of the period might speak for themselves about their reactions to that moment in time.

Thomas E. Leary
Elizabeth C. Sholes
Buffalo, New York
May 1998

One

IN THE BEGINNING

In the closing days of the 1895 Cotton States Centennial in Atlanta, Buffalo delegates Richmond C. Hill and John M. Brinker impulsively announced that their city would host an exposition in 1899. The invitation was reported by Atlanta newspapers but not in Buffalo. By 1897, however, the delegation pictured here at the Tennessee Centennial Exposition in Nashville founded the Pan-American Exposition Company and set the date for 1901. The company declared it would raise its capital privately, an unprecedented move. During 1898–1900, Congress, the President, the New York legislature, and the Common Council all provided endorsement and eventually some minimal funding while the company began selling stock then mortgage bonds to raise the estimated $5 million cost. Former expositions had been financially successful, and Buffalo projected 10 million visitors would attend. Promoters were ecstatic; they assured the public there was no financial risk and that "The Pan" would make Buffalo a "first-tier" city. Skeptics were dismissed. "The Pan" could not fail.

The third and final 25-member Board of Directors, dubbed a "collection of clubmen" by some, was elected by stockholders on March 7, 1899. Attorney John G. Milburn (left) became president. The board's primary function was fund-raising. They maintained committees for exhibits, construction, concessions, etc. but wisely hired professionals to run operations, including William I. Buchanan, former chief of agriculture at the Columbian Exposition. He became the Exposition's director general.

Banker and Exposition Treasurer George L. Williams (right) secured the first $2.5 million mortgage bond to supplement weak stock subscriptions. When construction began, directors had still not raised enough funds, and costs ran higher than estimated. A second mortgage was issued but was also insufficient. The directors did not worry; attendance was anticipated to fill the void through admissions and concessions. The deficit was ignored.

The Board of Women Managers was established in 1899 under Pres. Kate Hamlin. Some members were society matrons; others were professionals or active in social reform programs. Miss Marian DeForest (right), a newspaper reporter, became secretary. The women were trivialized by the press but were deeply involved in recruiting exhibitors, soliciting attendance by women's civic and professional organizations, and tirelessly promoting the Exposition at meetings throughout the country.

The Women Managers declared the Women's Building, the former Country Club, was not for exhibits. "Let women compete on equal terms with men in every department . . . This is what they want . . . not a classification which regards women's work as freakish." The building was open to all women, and while the managers entertained scores of guests, their goal was to provide a haven for the "New Woman" visitor to the Exposition.

11

In early spring of 1899, the most critical decision facing Pan-Am planners was the choice of a site for the Exposition. With opening day only two years away, little time remained for extended deliberations. The original site on Cayuga Island had been discarded as too remote from Buffalo; some 20 alternatives eventually surfaced, many intended to boost real estate development schemes. Local architects and engineers as well as consultants with national reputations pondered the problem. The leading contender at the outset was the Front, overlooking F.L. Olmsted's park system, Lake Erie, and the Niagara River. Consultants, including Daniel H. Burnham, chief of construction at the 1893 Chicago fair, favored the Front. "The first, broadest, and grandest natural beauty of Buffalo is that of the lake, which should be secured even at a considerable sacrifice of other advantages." This prospect also appealed to Buffalo architect George Cary shown here. Some influential members of Buffalo's elite, including Charles W. Goodyear and Frank B. Baird, backed Cary's vision for its great development potential after the Fair, including a prime location for a "permanent convention hall."

12

The Front's allure was undeniable: ". . . where is the man who doesn't like to look at the water and at boats?" queried one newspaper. However, problems subsequently appeared. Even reclaiming land as far south as Maryland or Georgia Streets would not have provided sufficient area. The partisan question of who would benefit from filling submerged lots was hotly debated. Both the New York Central Railroad's tracks and the Erie Canal—"sewage and all"—bisected the proposed site presenting major nuisances. "Dreams, dreams, nothing else," sighed one exasperated Pan-Am director. The plans of George and Thomas Cary seemed more suited to "a show of the size of the Hamburg Fair or the Toronto Exhibition . . ." At a stormy session on May 13, 1899, the board eventually voted in favor of the Rumsey Farm, shown here situated near other park lands between Elmwood, Delaware, and Forest Avenues and the New York Central Belt Line. The tract possessed fewer scenic advantages but also far fewer difficulties; moreover, "In order to reach the grounds by driving, riding, or walking, the City's best section would be traversed."

Designing an Exposition demanded imaginative work under severe time constraints; the accomplishments of predecessors provided standards to be emulated if not imitated. The benchmark was the 1893 Columbian Exposition; its neo-classical Court of Honor, "The White City," borrowed from the 1889 Paris Fair, had opened new vistas of architectural symbolism and urban beautification, although architect Louis Sullivan thought the monumental spectacle derivative. Buffalo's pockets were not as deep as Chicago's, and there was a ". . . desire to avoid reminiscences of the Chicago Exposition." The job of guiding Buffalo fell to the Chair of the Board of Architects, John Merven Carrère. Recommended by Daniel Burnham, Carrère was a relatively young man whose firm had recently won the competition to design the New York Public Library and had conjured up some exotic hotels in Florida for developer Henry Flagler. Other members of the architectural board included New Yorkers Walter Cook and John Galen Howard; Bostonians George F. Shepley and R.S. Peabody; and three locals, George Cary, Edward B. Green, and August C. Esenwein. They first met on June 17, 1899, and presented preliminary designs August 22.

The task of translating designs into construction plans and specifications fell to the architectural bureau within the Department of Works. Supervising architect Henry S. Kissam and his successors, along with Chief Draftsman Henry H. Weatherwax, headed this unit housed in the Service Building, the first structure constructed. The advisory Board of Architects had presented initial plans in August, but changes and refinements continued to trickle in throughout the fall and winter.

The Exposition incorporated women in professional capacities. Architect Josephine Wright Chapman (left) won a sealed competition in Boston to design the New England Building, and S. Cecilia Cotter (right) displayed her sculpture in Fine Arts. Ethnology engaged several professionals, including Director Benedict's assistants Katherine Randall and Josephine Lewis, and Claire Shuttleworth who provided some exhibit artwork. Numerous other women contributed to the Exposition's operations as technical, office, and service employees.

In his New York studio, Charles Yardley Turner and his assistants worked out a novel architectural color scheme blending aesthetics with early anthropology. Turner selected his hues from a palette tinged with evolutionary theories from Social Darwinism. Primary colors signified primitive conditions; pastels represented the apex of civilization. Progress was expressed by reducing contrasts as visitors approached the Electric Tower (model at right) from the Triumphal Bridge.

Adelaide Thorpe was Turner's assistant director of Interior Decoration. Her use of cloth walls and ceiling swags established the tone for each building using national flags and booth colors to create overall impressions. Once colors were selected, no exhibitor was allowed to conflict with her choices. This marked a departure from the Columbian Exposition, where building framework had been left exposed and central control over individual exhibit design was absent.

Many of the engineers in charge of building the Pan-Am were veterans of earlier fairs at Chicago and Omaha. Director of Works Newcomb Carlton, seated center, occupied the functional equivalent of Daniel Burnham's position as *generalissimo* of the Columbian Exposition. Just 30 years old, Carlton was a graduate of Stevens Institute of Technology; as a mechanical engineer he represented the growing branch of the profession that was trained through formal education rather than in shops and factories. Unlike many of his subordinates, Carlton had no background in erecting transient temples of commerce and culture on greenfield sites, but prior to his appointment he had enjoyed a good working relationship with Exposition President Milburn. Landscape architect Rudolph Ulrich, seated second from left, had been responsible for seeding, sodding, and nurturing trees, shrubs, and plants in Chicago and Omaha. Consulting electrical engineer Luther Stieringer (seated far right) and Chief of the Mechanical and Electrical Bureau Henry Rustin (standing, second from right) could both call on extensive experience with illuminating large fairs. Rustin's experience in Omaha was an important asset to Buffalo.

17

Preliminary work preparing the Rumsey site for construction commenced on May 18, 1899, when engineer George A. Ricker and his assistants undertook a topographical survey. However, negotiations over the Rumsey property lease dragged on into the fall; work on groundbreaking and fencing did not get underway until September 26. This October 2 photograph shows men and horse-drawn teams removing topsoil for subsequent grading and landscaping. The line of poplars defines Amherst Street.

During 1900, the construction agenda included driving pilings for foundations and enclosing the structures so they could withstand the winter of 1900–1901 before exhibit installation in the spring. This view shows the site of the Machinery and Transportation Building along the south side of Amherst Street as of May 2, 1900. Flooring is being laid atop the pilings. The poplar trees would become part of the sunken garden along the West Mall.

The Department of Works Landscape Bureau was turning the site into a garden. Nurseries such as Ellwanger & Barry of Rochester, New York furnished ornamental trees and shrubs. Other greenery was propagated in the Exposition's own nursery or transplanted from Stony Point, future site of the Lackawanna Steel Company. That company's cheap land purchase was connived for them by Exposition directors Milburn and John Albright pretending to be looking for a Pan-Am site.

Water features were an important facet of the overall design. A canal about a mile in length encircled the central groups of buildings. This artificial waterway broadened into a pair of small ponds on the southern perimeter called East and West Mirror Lakes. The canals were 30–50 feet wide with water 3.5–10 feet deep. The finished banks were lined with sheet piling then sodded and landscaped. The canal bottom consisted of crushed stone.

On July 19, 1900, William Goldie & Sons Company was using the vertical boiler and steam engine in the center of this photograph to hoist the transverse roof trusses of the Machinery Building into place. The Howe-type truss spanned the distance between the lattice columns on the left and the bearing wall on the right. Additional composite wood-and-metal trusses (foreground) were assembled and were awaiting their turn.

As of December 7, 1900, both the framework construction and the exterior covering of the Agriculture Building were well in hand. The interior consisted of a main longitudinal hall with parallel side aisles. Intermediate rows of columns supported the principal roof trusses which spanned 97 feet. These columns were built up of Norway pine planks bolted and spiked together, and supported on piles that also carried the flooring system.

On December 5, 1900, the Temple of Music still lacked its decorative skin. The building's framework consisted of wooden members with cast-iron connections and steel tension rods. The structure included examples of heavy timber construction techniques that interested engineers. The interior featured an octagonal auditorium with a domed ceiling. The space beneath the exterior roof dome was not accessible to the public; it contained supporting trusses, light shafts, and a ventilator.

By February 16, 1901, the Temple of Music was sprouting a profusion of sculpture and other surface details. Completing such specimens of "occasional architecture" required the skills of specialized contractors: foundation work, carpentry, plaster and staff work, figure modeling, metal roofing, and painting. To economize, on July 16, 1900, the Exposition's Executive Committee had awarded the Temple of Music carpentry job to John Feist for $55,000—$16,588 less than his original bid.

Sculpture for the buildings and grounds represented artistry and mass production. Director of Sculpture Karl Bitter, a native of Vienna, employed as many as one hundred workmen in his studios in Weehawken and Hoboken, New Jersey. The majority of the artisans were Italian; they churned out five hundred pieces of statuary in five months. To accelerate the process, Bitter utilized a "pointing machine" invented by Robert T. Payne that mechanically enlarged sculptor's small models.

This mammoth eagle took shape in contractor James Alexander's Buffalo workshops rather than Bitter's studio. John Frederickson labored three weeks and used a ton of clay in fashioning this model. Eight staff copies that simulated marble were to perch around the dome of the Ethnology Building. As in iron founding, models were used as patterns to make molds in which liquid staff mixtures took their final shape.

This photograph shows workmen applying precast staff panels to window arches in the Machinery Building. Staff consisted of plaster-of-Paris mixed with hemp fibers as a binder. Contractor Joseph Eastman had concocted this recipe to facilitate rapid construction of temporary ornamentation at the 1893 Chicago Fair. Like wood, staff could be shaped and painted in numerous ways. Many skilled craftsmen emigrated from Europe to help build American expositions.

A staff and plastering crew surveys its handiwork of embellishing skeleton columns and other wooden framing elements in the Midway entrances. In August 1900, seven hundred staff workers had struck Smith & Eastman and other contractors but failed to gain the desired wage increase. Plaster and staff workers walked out again in January 1901, this time over whether they or the sculpture modelers working under Bitter's deputy, Carl Bell, should repoint statuary.

Unlike other principal exposition buildings, the Electric Tower, the Fair's centerpiece, was built around a structural steel framework. Different construction methods were therefore required, and conditions on the job site also varied. On November 1, 1900, a carpenter escaped injury when a heavy steel punch was knocked off a staging and narrowly missed his head. As the tower climbed skyward one observer noted, ". . . you strain your eyes looking up to the dizzy heights where the men at work on the tower are erecting the great steel trusses of this tall structure. At a height of 300 feet they walk around upon the beams as unconcernedly as if they were not ten feet above terra firma." The loftiness of the structure also affected labor negotiations at the end of November. Union ironworkers demanded the promised wage increase for work over 200 feet. As in Chicago, strikes and accidents punctuated the period of construction. Union hiring practices and wages generally prevailed among the building trades, but work was still driven ahead at "railroad pressure."

24

On May 2, 1900, a spontaneous strike erupted among unorganized immigrant day laborers employed by the Exposition Company and some contractors. The workers' objective was an eight-hour day that had supposedly been established by the Labor Registration Bureau that regulated hiring under a compromise agreement with local trade unions. The strikers soon returned to work, but on May 7 the Executive Committee conceded and recommended an eight-hour day for Exposition laborers.

The hurricane that had devastated Galveston, Texas struck Buffalo on September 12, 1900. On the Midway, the Streets of Venice (above), and the Trip to the Moon showed the effects of the 78-mph winds. More serious casualties included the U.S. Government Building and the Electricity Building, where one of the towers toppled. The Midway and Stadium restaurants also suffered damage to their towers. Luckily, no one on the grounds was injured.

On March 1, 1901, with opening day two months away, Midway buildings remained unfinished; many exhibits awaited installation. In the latter task, the design of the grounds was no asset, as Director-General Buchanan realized, ". . . the raised position given the entire central portion of the Exposition as an architectural necessity . . . embarrassed the rapid movement of exhibits and materials owing to the sharp inclines at all bridge entrances."

The crew of the big guns already installed near the U.S. Government buildings could enjoy a brief respite on April 11, 1901, while other exhibitors scrambled to install their displays. Heavy wagons hauling exhibits continually chewed up temporary roadways. In late May the *New York Times* reported, "Many of the streets have not yet been paved" while "Many important exhibits are not yet ready." Chicago had experienced similar problems.

Two

THE RAINBOW CITY

The Pan-Am's designers viewed the Rumsey farm as a blank slate. "The site in itself offered no features which were characteristic of the city of Buffalo or of the locality, such as a site along the lake-front might have given . . ." John M. Carrère and his team had to devise a comprehensive vision of the buildings and grounds as well as attend to myriad details. Given limited topographical and financial resources, the design group steered a middle course between the experimental features of the 1900 Paris Exposition and the neo-classical grandeur of 1893 Chicago. Buffalo's overall plan earned praise from contemporary critics, but many bedeviling errors marred its accomplishments. The architects did not consult with the exhibits department and vice versa; as a result, there was insufficient space for many displays, and several ancillary facilities had to be constructed. Karl Bitter's sculpture plan and C.Y. Turner's color scheme both carried messages about the relative superiority of western civilization compared to other cultures; however, it is not clear how well visitors absorbed these perspectives.

27

The Pan-American Exposition *Art Hand-Book* recommended that "The first visit to the Exposition, if possible, should be made through the Lincoln Parkway entrance which is the 'front door' of the Exposition." John M. Carrère preferred this route "to obtain a gradual transition from the natural scenery of the Park . . . into the formal setting of the Exposition." Unfortunately, numerous visitors did not use this entry; it was not served by mass transit.

The Pan-American
as viewed from the
Hotel Alcazar.

People arriving on streetcars and the Belt Line railway entered via the West Amherst gate or other points; they plunged immediately into the midst of the attractions. According to critic Herbert Croly, ". . . visitors who did not approach by way of the Park and lane . . . would not have been led to the splendid effects of the Court of the Fountains by successive and inevitable stages . . . Tourists would have stumbled upon them unawares."

Routes from the Lincoln Parkway Gate, Water Gate, Meadow Gate, and Elmwood Gate converged at the Approach to the Forecourt and the Triumphal Bridge. From this vantage point looking north, the preferred vista of the principal axis and buildings including the Electric Tower, began to unfold "like a flower." The aggregate length of the Approach, Forecourt, and Bridge (also known as the Triumphal Causeway) was 1,000 feet.

The gigantic causeway spanning Mirror Lake commemorated "the triumph of America over tyranny and despotism," but an unmistakable whiff of imperial grandeur clung to the structure. Carrere and Director of Sculpture Karl Bitter collaborated on the Triumphal Bridge design which Bitter claimed, ". . . will excel the famous Alexandrian Bridge at Paris," erected for the 1900 World's Fair. Some observers, however, felt that the bridge was grossly out of scale with its surroundings.

After crossing the Triumphal Bridge, visitors reached the intersection of the Exposition's two principal axes, forming an inverted T. The cross arm, running east and west, was known as the Esplanade. Curved pergolas, Carrère's adaptation of Pompeiian garden trellises, functioned as open-air restaurants. The vertical stem of the T, centered around the Court of the Fountains (right foreground), ran north past the Electric Tower to the Propylaea.

This view looks south from the Electric Tower to the Court of Fountains, the Esplanade, and the Triumphal Bridge. The perspective reveals the predilection for monumental symmetrical compositions shared by Beaux Arts–trained architects, such as Carrère and R.S. Peabody, regardless of any particular style. This central court occupied a larger area than either of the comparable spaces at the Chicago or Paris expositions.

Along the western Esplanade the theme unifying the design elements celebrated the bounty of earth's exploitable resources. The Horticulture Building overlooked the Fountain of Nature. Glass-roofed arcades linked Horticulture with the Mines and Graphic Arts buildings in a semi-circular group. Designed by R.S. Peabody's Boston firm, which had grafted Spanish references onto the Columbian Exposition's Machinery Hall, the Buffalo complex also evoked the Italian Renaissance.

Balancing the Horticulture group were the U.S. Government facilities around the eastern Esplanade; their thematic thread traced the evolution of civic institutions. J. Knox Taylor, a federal employee and not part of Carrère's team, designed the government pavilions. The Exposition's *Art Hand-Book* declared that Taylor's work "more than any other on the grounds is Spanish-American in its architecture." Nevertheless he ignored Turner's color scheme and substituted his own.

Between the Esplanade on the south and the Mall to the north, the Ethnology Building (far right) and the Manufactures and Liberal Arts Building (left) fronted on the Court of the Fountains. Along with the Machinery Building on the opposite side of this principal north-south axis, the 350 x 500-foot Manufactures Building was one of the largest exhibit spaces at the Pan-Am; it would have been dwarfed by its gargantuan 787 x 1,687-foot counterpart in Chicago, planned by George B. Post to surpass Paris' 1889 *Palais des Machines* as the largest building in the world. George Foster Shepley of Boston designed the Buffalo version. His firm, Shepley, Rutan & Coolidge had continued the architectural practice of the deceased luminary Henry Hobson Richardson, Shepley being Richardson's son-in-law. The Manufactures Building turned a rather restrained facade to the Court of the Fountains so as not to compete with the Electric Tower. The balustrades and other garnishes around the Grand Basin echoed the formal treatment given to the White City's basin by Henry C. Codman of Frederick Law Olmsted's landscaping firm.

Buildings along the west side of the Court of the Fountains included, from north to south: the Temple of Music (left foreground), Machinery and Transportation (left center), and Electricity (right center). Also visible are the twin towers of the Midway Restaurant as well as portions of the Propylaea and the Electric Tower (far right background). This perspective reveals the "picturesque ensemble on a formal ground plan" that Carrère and his colleagues aspired to create by controlling groupings of building masses and open spaces while permitting considerable liberty in the development of individual features. Carrère thought such an approach could improve the design of American cities in ways that the monotonous monumentality of the White City had not anticipated. The orthodox architectural critic Mrs. Schuyler Van Rensselaer concurred. "After the beauty of this great court has been appreciated it is well to study its ground-plan on paper. There could be no better lesson in the art of securing variety in unity."

August Esenwein's Temple of Music would have appalled Sir Nikolaus Pevsner, an eminent architectural historian and no fan of the elaborate decorations covering many Spanish buildings. Pevsner identified the diffusion of Islamic ornamentation by *mudejares*, Moslems conquered by medieval Christians, as one factor in the persistence of rich architectural carving in Spain. He linked this trend to the Plateresque styling of the Renaissance and the baroque fantasies of the brothers Churriguera.

Author Herbert Croly found the music hall's high-relief sculpture unpalatable, ". . . these ornamental details, in themselves altogether too prominent, were further emphasized by the application of various tawdry colors." Another journalist, Walter Hines Page, recoiled from the building's hues including "violent Pompeiian red on a general scheme of salmon." Many commentators debated the aesthetic merits of Turner's polychrome treatment without dwelling on its ideological dimensions and cultural stereotypes.

The Ethnology Building, a classical and Renaissance confection, was paired with the Temple of Music to mark the transition from the Esplanade to the Court of the Fountains. The architect of Ethnology was George Cary of Buffalo whose resume included study at Harvard, Columbia, and the *École des Beaux-Arts*. His local practice commenced in 1890 and included commissions for the University of Buffalo and Buffalo General Hospital.

This newspaper sketch satirized some visitors' disorientation in the Ethnology Building. "If you want to see the world go round, come rapidly down the spiral stairs from the gallery." Ascending color gradations around that staircase signaled mankind's rise from savagery to civilization. However, during the Gilded Age, alienated intellectuals such as Henry Adams wondered whether the evolution of the presidency from George Washington to Ulysses S. Grant represented progress or decline.

35

Neither Edward B. Green nor William B. Wicks had been exposed to the Beaux-Arts training common among several of the other Pan-Am architects. Both had merely studied at Cornell. Nevertheless, their Buffalo firm, Green & Wicks, also clothed building exteriors in eclectic historical styles. Their Machinery and Transportation Building resembled a Moorish *alcazar*, a type of fortified residence with a central patio and angled pavilions that represented vestigial castle towers.

In the Machinery Building, Green & Wicks' patio had to be roofed over to create additional display space. A pumping station for the Exposition's fountains was situated in the basement of the interior court. One engine's manufacturer, miffed at this arrangement, complained to *American Machinist*, "The engines are down in a hole, and there is nothing to indicate that the hole exists, nor that it contains an engine exhibit."

36

A landscaped area called the Court of Lilies separated the Machinery Building from the Temple of Music and the Graphic Arts Building to the south. This court was flanked by terraces defined by a trellis with Grecian caryatids and by a free-standing Corinthian colonnade, shown here. The surroundings of the lake at Parc Monceau in Paris inspired Carrère's treatment of these combined resting places and elevated vantage points.

This view shows some of the ensemble of architectural, sculptural, and aquatic features grouped around the Court of the Fountains. Looking southeast from the Grand Basin, a portion of the Manufactures and Liberal Arts Building (left) appears next to a colonnade in the Court of Cypresses near the Ethnology Building. The sculpture in the foreground is the Birth of Venus. Herbert Croly particularly enjoyed this "charming and delightful" perspective.

37

The south entrance of Green & Wicks' Electricity Building incorporated several features characteristic of the Spanish Renaissance. Towers with octagonal belfries flanked an elaborately embellished frontispiece including an ornamental arch with supporting columns. Spanish elevational design of this period had emphasized the aedicular treatment of openings that incorporated doorways and windows within a common vertical framework of richly carved motifs as devices for punctuating the facade.

McKim, Mead & White's 1893 Agricultural Building was described as "one of the most aggressively Roman structures of the Fair." By contrast, Shepley, Rutan & Coolidge's Agriculture Building at the Pan-Am offered a restrained variation on the Spanish theme of the Fair. Regarding its coloring, one guidebook observed, "The scheme which elsewhere has been a quasi-success, seems here to have been a marked success." The building also boasted an escalator.

The Mall formed a secondary east-west axis along the former Amherst Street. This view looks east across the canal from between the Bazaar (left foreground) and the Acetylene Building (right foreground). A sunken garden separated the Electricity Building (left) from Machinery and Transportation (right). The poplar trees in the sunken garden defined the original Amherst Street grade, indicating the extent of fill required for the Exposition's construction.

The Plaza served as a transitional area between the major Exposition buildings and the railroad lines north of the grounds. Walter Cook (another Beaux-Arts alumnus), designed the square and its surrounding buildings. The Plaza was "treated as a small Court of Honor." One critic dubbed it "the backyard of the Exposition." The space included a bandstand and sunken garden, concessionaire pavilions, restaurants, and entrances to the Midway and Stadium.

The Electric Tower represented the culmination of the architectural composition grouped around the Esplanade, the Court of Fountains, the Mall, and the Plaza. The Pan-Am's focal point and signature structure evolved from a proposal by Chicago concessionaire David R. Proctor who wanted to outdo the Eiffel Tower, built for the 1889 Exposition in Paris. Proctor envisioned a steel-framed observation tower 1,152 feet high. Thirty-three elevators would whisk the intrepid public up to one of seven landings including an artificial ice skating rink 675 feet in the air. Given the Fair's celebration of Niagara's electric power, Proctor was also prepared to illuminate his gargantuan creation. The Committee on Concessions received several other tower proposals besides Proctor's, including one from Buffalo architect Robert Reidpath. Eventually the task of combining the features of an observation tower with an electric tower was handed to John Galen Howard, president of the Beaux-Arts Society of New York. His firm Howard, Cauldwell & Morgan, had finished as runner-up to Carrère & Hastings in the recent New York Library competition.

While considerably smaller than Proctor's original proposal, the Electric Tower still dominated the fairgrounds. Howard's conception underwent several alterations. The final form resembled a tall office building with a steel framework concealed beneath a skin of staff and a rash of historical ornamentation, much like many skyscrapers of this period. One guidebook noted, ". . . the tower cannot be said to have been designed in any strictly defined traditional 'style.' "

Statuary and aquatic spectacle celebrated the harnessing of Niagara's cataracts for hydroelectric power generation. Julian Hawthorne of *Cosmopolitan* resorted to Biblical analogies when describing the cascade gushing from the Electric Tower. "A sort of miracle seems to have been accomplished, as when Moses smote the rock for the thirsty Israelites . . . from every point of view it is visible, and the soft thunder of its down-tumbling rejoices the soul."

The Fountain of Nature on the West Esplanade illustrated the Pan-Am sculptors' penchant for allegory, the representation of abstract concepts through concrete images. George T. Brewster of New York used human figures as symbols of Mother Nature, the Four Elements, the Four Seasons, and the Four Winds. Other thematically linked statuary in this section included Animal Wealth, Floral Wealth, Mineral Wealth, and the Fountain of Ceres, the harvest goddess.

Sculpture groups arranged on the East Esplanade presented unsubtle messages about the evolutionary development of western political and cultural institutions. Posed before the U.S. Government buildings, "aboriginal warriors" in John J. Boyle's, the Savage Age (south group), were depicted abducting a woman. Boyle also used Goths from the Dark Ages to represent his belief that society required organized religion and legal codes to control human impulses toward random violence.

Karl Bitter was not shy about proclaiming the pedagogical purpose of exposition sculpture. He saw his overall plan as a "sermon" that would employ fine art to elevate public understanding of history while also improving popular taste. Along the Court of the Fountains, Bitter's didactic script celebrated man's increasing ability to manipulate the natural environment through the technologies and products arrayed in nearby buildings such as Machinery and Manufactures.

A. Phimister Proctor's jumbo genre groups, Agriculture (shown above) and Manufacture (shown here) were to be removed from the Court of the Fountains because they were too large. Several critics said, "There was an excess instead of a dearth of sculpture scattered throughout the Exposition grounds," much of it characterized by "conventional symbolism." The structure and effect of Bitter's plan was lost on visitors who did not enter via the Triumphal Bridge.

The buildings of the various states and nations represented at the Exposition were grouped in the southeast quadrant of the grounds near the Triumphal Bridge. This view looks west from the Indian Mound toward the Ohio Building (right) and the Illinois Building (left). The state buildings complex was not planned as a component of the formal architectural scheme, and Director-General Buchanan regretted the relatively isolated location of the site.

Many of the individual state buildings echoed architectural styles different from the various Spanish motifs adopted by the Board of Architects. Josephine Wright Chapman's New England States Building with its colossal Ionic portico and rooftop balustrade reflected a typical regional rediscovery of discarded precedents that would eventually be bundled into popular period revivals. Construction of the state buildings began very late, and many were left unfinished until mid-June.

The Mexican Building served as the headquarters of its national commission whose professionalism impressed Director-General Buchanan. Only exhibits related to mining were housed here; other displays were located in the Manufactures, Agriculture, Horticulture, and Ethnology buildings. Buffalo newspapers praised Mexican Pres. Porfirio Diaz profusely; his policies catered to expanding investments by domestic and international capital. In 1911, a revolution would topple the dictatorial Diaz.

Among the state and foreign pavilions, Ecuador possessed one of the more flamboyant variations on the Spanish-Colonial architectural theme. Designed by the New York architectural firm of James & Leo, this building was "noticeable by its high gable and Queen Anne style of outline," according to a contemporary guidebook. Other details included rusticated portico columns, a central octagonal tower, and multiple roof lines clad in the ubiquitous imitation red tiles.

The marble walls of the New York State Building were designed to outlast the Pan-Am's plaster palaces. Architect George Cary transplanted the Greek Doric style of the Parthenon from the Acropolis to the slope overlooking Delaware Park Lake. In 1902, this temple of culture became the home of the Buffalo Historical Society and still serves that purpose, though Mrs. Harry Paine Whitney's statue of Aspiration no longer greets visitors.

During the Fair, the New York State Building housed no exhibits. The Grand Court and other first-floor areas functioned as reception rooms where fatigued tourists could collapse onto mission furniture and contemplate the elegant interior. Various groups also held meetings in the building. Paintings occupied the upstairs galleries. Though not ready for occupancy until mid-summer, a total of 118,554 people passed through the building and signed the visitors' registers.

Three

THE CITY ELECTRIC

Nocturnal illumination of the Pan-Am buildings and grounds created a memorable experience for visitors. In the words of one observer the phenomenon was ". . . the great popular 'card' of the Exposition and probably did more to advertise it than any other single attraction." Lighting became a design feature because of the recent electrical engineering innovations at Niagara Falls: generation of alternating current and its transmission over a considerable distance to Buffalo in 1896. According to a writer for the technical journal, *Machinery*, "No such spectacle would be attempted anywhere else in the world at the present day. No such extravagant outlay of lights would be thought of where the power had to be furnished by coal and steam." Though hydroelectric power was transmitted greater distances in other regions such as California at the time of the Pan-Am, Buffalo still stood at the threshold of a new era in the industrial and domestic applications of this novel power source. *Harper's Weekly* stated "Electrical Niagara is going to make Buffalo one of the largest manufacturing centers in the world."

The hydraulic turbines and generators of the Niagara Falls Power Company supplied five thousand hp. for exterior illumination using incandescent lamps. The 25-cycle frequency alternating current was initially generated at 2,200 volts and was transformed to 22,000 volts for transmission to Buffalo over copper and aluminum lines. At the terminal station on Ontario Street in Buffalo, the voltage was reduced to 11,000.

From Ontario Street copper wires led to the rheostat house on the fairgrounds, 650 feet north of the West Amherst gate. Three water rheostats controlled the current so that exterior incandescent lamps could be brought up to full glow over an 80-second period, thus creating the Pan-Am's most spectacular visual effect. Transformers in the Electricity Building (above) subsequently dropped the voltage from 11,000 to 1,800 for further distribution.

The distributing switchboard was also located in the northwest corner of the Electricity Building, adjacent to the transformers. Hand-operated switches controlled the supply of current through feeder circuits to numerous transformer pits throughout the fairgrounds. Equipment in these pits further reduced the voltage from 1,800 to 104 for the small incandescent lamps. The water rheostats could likewise be operated from this area, which formed part of General Electric's exhibit.

The exteriors of the buildings were first illuminated at 4:30 p.m. on December 7, 1900. On the 28th of that month, Henry Rustin, chief of the Electrical and Mechanical Bureau, lit up the Machinery Building so that Exposition photographer C.D. Arnold could take some publicity shots. Arnold professed satisfaction with his three exposures. His night photographs at the Pan-Am required leaving the shutter open for 25 minutes.

Lights had burned at night on fairgrounds prior to the Pan-Am. However, the electrical engineers at Buffalo refined the experience gained at earlier expositions. Rustin, a veteran of the 1898 Omaha Fair, believed, ". . . the secret of successful illumination is uniformity in distribution of light." He preferred the smaller incandescent bulbs visible on the standards in this photograph to the arc lights or other methods that caused a disconcerting glare.

Niagara's alternating current chiefly fueled the decorative exterior lighting. A power plant located near the northwest corner of the grounds contained second-hand equipment to generate direct current for some machinery exhibits, the Midway buildings, and for arc light installations. On July 29, 1901, the Midway was plunged into darkness. Numerous amusement proprietors had to refund money to patrons. Concessionaires sought compensation for their losses from the Exposition Company.

As twilight settled over the Exposition grounds each evening, crowds eagerly awaited the gradual brightening of the lights controlled by the rheostats. *The World's Work* correspondent, Walter Hines Page described the ceremony. "You have hardly realized the scene as it appears in the dusk, when on the rows of posts tiny dots of light appear in clusters, like little pink buds in a nosegay. Then the pink points grow brighter and change their hue, and in another moment the full illumination bursts forth, and the whole great court becomes luminous with a soft brilliancy that does not tire the eye. And it is a new kind of brilliancy. You are face to face with the most magnificent and artistic nocturnal scene that man has ever made." Page went on to tell readers, "I had the pleasure to see this illumination first in the company of a child of 10 years. She stood for a minute in speechless wonder. Then she cried, 'Oh, isn't it beautiful!' And she danced in forgetfulness of herself and asked, 'Is it really real?'"

Like the architectural design, the color scheme, and the sculpture plan, the nightly illumination was best viewed from a particular vantage point. "If possible the visitor should arrange to see the Exposition first in the evening, arriving at the Triumphal Causeway a few minutes before the lights are lit. The effect produced by the gradual turning on of the electrical current is the crowning triumph of the Exposition."

Even fireworks paled by comparison with the dazzling display of light around the Court of Fountains. William Drysdale, the cynical *New York Times* reporter, offered the opinion that "It is a stroke of genius on somebody's part that the lights are all turned off about the middle of the evening and then suddenly turned on so that no one need spend an entire evening on the grounds."

Opening day May 1 lights went on at 7:20 p.m. The schedule advanced two minutes each evening until reaching 8 p.m. Thereafter the moment of illumination decreased by two minutes per night. As of October 1 lighting up occurred at 6 p.m. Lights were usually turned off at 11 p.m. This view shows the Fountain of Abundance with the Temple of Music in the background.

Finley Peter Dunne, a famous humorist of the period, commented on the Pan-Am's nightly illumination through his Irish saloonkeeper character Mr. Dooley and his cronies. " 'The sun is settin' earlier,' says he to Connors. 'Since th' fair begun,' says Connors, 'it hasn't showed afther eight o'clock. We seldom hear iv it nowadays. We set our clocks be th' risin' an' settin' iv th' lights.' "

On July 31, Thomas Edison watched the regular evening illumination from the Esplanade. "This is the apotheosis of incandescent light," exclaimed the Wizard of Menlo Park whose fame was due in part to developing that type of filament lamp. Earlier, Edison, whose interests also included magnetic ore separation processes, had viewed the exhibits in the Mines Building (above). He concluded his visit by sampling the attractions on the Midway.

Three weeks after Edison's benediction, lights in Manufactures and Liberal Arts and throughout the grounds failed for nearly two hours in "the most serious accident that has befallen the Exposition in some time." Visitors were "groping about in Stygian darkness." Most of the crowd made its way to the West Amherst gate. According to newspaper reports, "the trouble was with the Haversaw cable" that officials finally bypassed with the safety cable.

The Pan-Am was staged during an era of massive business mergers, dizzying technological change, and serious labor conflicts. *Century* editor Richard Watson Gilder composed inscriptions flanking the Machinery Building's east entrance that attempted to invoke a spirit of harmony between capitalists and workers. Despite this noble rhetoric, electrician Frank Kinsley suffered grievous burns on July 30 from a fire in the nearby transformer substation.

Even the official Exposition guidebook conceded that, ". . . the ordinary visitor will certainly find himself more inclined to study the wonderful freedom and beauty of the decorations than to go seriously into the evidence they give of the progress of electrical science." Diversions abounded around the Plaza (above) including the Midway amusements and the athletic events at the Stadium, "a gigantic son of Madison Square Garden with its hat off."

Julian Hawthorne of *Cosmopolitan* interpreted the Electric Tower as the symbol of a new world order as well as a technological achievement. "This Tower, too, being dedicated to light, which is, spiritually interpreted, the genius of our age, indicates that all Americans shall be one in virtue of the inevitable influence of the understanding, that enlightened economic perception which lights the way for the warmth and substance of mutual affection and trust. The Tower of Light is the tower of peace and good will, whose turrets already appear above the horizons of the future. Science, discovery, and industry are the great, immortal democrats whose teaching shall wipe out political boundaries, and heal national jealousies, and sweep hitherto hostile units into the great current of a commonweal. Monarchies and oligarchies cannot prevail against them, for they find a place for every man and bring him to it in freedom and self-respect. We shall have all America united; and what America becomes is the prototype of what the world must be."

56

Mrs. Harriet Taggart Mack, member of the Board of Women Managers, recorded in her diary an impression more personal but no less cosmic than Julian Hawthorne's vision. "When people saw the Electric Tower lighted, starting from tiny jewels of light, to culminate in a tremendous force of light, they were frequently awed and gave way to tears. It was a sublime spectacle. No exposition has ever had anything so beautiful as the Pan-American Electric Tower. Never again will Buffalonians see on this earth such an inspiring and heavenly sight—the band playing 'Nearer My God to Thee' as it gradually unfolded against the darkness of the sky to throw its beaming light to the world. It was as if God spoke." Herbert Croly of *The Architectural Record* was more inclined to nit-pick: ". . . the illumination was startlingly novel and brilliant, but if it is possible for any future exposition to use the same amount of light, perhaps better results can be obtained by freeing the plan of the illuminations from such a scrupulous adherence to architectural outlines."

One of the *National Magazine* reporters greatly appreciated the accomplishments of the architects, painters, sculptors, landscapers, and engineers who had collaborated to create an extraordinary ambiance. "It seems like a glimpse into another world or at least a foretaste of the glories of another century . . . the outlines of the buildings traced in the rows of electric

lights, the softening colors and brilliant play of glass and gilding, and the reflection of this fairyland in the surrounding waters; the jeweled spray of cascade and fountain, and the almost spiritual beauty of group and statue, form a picture that can never be forgotten. Standing on the Triumphal Bridge as the darkness closes and looking upon the scene—the effect is thrilling."

Due to dramatic breakthroughs and incremental improvements, the pace of technological change around 1901 converted yesterday's innovations into historical curiosities. As *The World's Work* reminded its readers, "Visitors to Chicago in 1893 will recall the electrical fountain which played at one end of the Court of Honor, producing brilliant colored effects in water. Electric lighting has since that time been so highly developed as a fine art that such concentrated fountain-effects are now regarded as 'shows.' They do not fit into a scheme of general illumination. The electrical fountain at Buffalo, therefore, which is much more elaborate than the one at Chicago was, has been put far off from the court on an island in the lake at the southern end of the grounds. There it is a spectacle by itself." The electrical engineering consultant, Luther Steiringer, was enthusiastic about the opportunity that the Pan-Am had provided for professionals in his field to demonstrate their prowess. "We have now done what I have long wished for a chance to do."

Four

PROGRESS ON DISPLAY

Exhibits were the heart of the Pan-Am. Promoting material achievements of Western progress was the rationale for all expositions, but U.S. conquests in the 1898 Spanish-American War offered a special opportunity to flout the nation's colonial superiority. Director-General Buchanan noted that Latin-American exhibits were predominantly of natural resources "especially those . . . which awaited development." U.S. agriculture and mineral resources were also overshadowed by capital and consumer goods and by evidence of imperial conquest, all boldly displayed before admiring visitors. True global manufacturing was virtually non-existent, and Republican and business tariff policies actively prohibited "free" trade. Thus U.S. manufacturers seized every opportunity to present their wares to an international audience of potential buyers. Buffalo-based Larkin Company made and sold soap. It also developed the premium system; there was virtually nothing one could not buy from Larkin catalogues with coupons obtained from soap purchases. Their exhibit included model rooms completely furnished with Larkin premiums as well as displays of soap production. Larkin represented everything U.S. ingenuity could manufacture and sell.

Power was fundamental to the Pan-American. Steam and gas boilers and engines were selected for both utility and display. Higgins the mover transported many of these machines to the fairgrounds. For each operating engine, the Exposition provided space, a foundation, fuel, and an engineer at $3.50 per day. However, steam did little to power exhibits "for electricity sets all the machinery in motion."

Capital machinery and heavy equipment was shown mainly in the Machinery and Transportation Building. Products were displayed with flair: Norton Emery Wheel's 1-ton Romanesque columns were made from their own grinding wheels. Amid this spurious refinement, the Worcester, Massachusetts company operated cutters, grinders, and other tools, ever mindful that the point of the display was to sell their wares.

The L & I.J. White Company, founded in Buffalo in 1837, was prominently located in the Machinery Building. Amid flags, swags, and golden eagles with electrified ruby eyes, the company displayed its large assortment of cutting tools including firemen's axes, machine knives, ice cutters' tools, chisels, saws, butchers' equipment, and other products for industry. The highlight was the Big Knife, which was one of the "sights" of the Machinery Building's south wall.

The Acetylene Building was built in part by a woman carpenter, Ida Churchyard. Journalist Arthur Goodrich said of the isolated site, "The building is looked upon with a certain amount of awe . . . for the impression of danger is connected closely with acetylene in the popular mind." It was nevertheless useful. Abner Acetylene Gas Co. from Chicago displayed gas-powered electric-light generators with automatic feed systems that could illuminate from 10 to 20,000 lights.

The sheer abundance of machines led *Cosmopolitan* magazine to comment, "The eye becomes tired and the imagination sated by the plethora of cogs and blades, wheels and dynamos." Although the array of devices and gadgets was confusing to many visitors, the author noted that exhibits such as that from Pittsburgh's Westinghouse Company in the Electricity Building "stirs our pulses with pride, even if we gape at it with unenlightened eyes."

The Standard Paint gazebo, called the P&B Building, came to Buffalo directly from the 1900 Paris World's Fair. The enclosure was itself part of the exhibit, featuring the New York City company's paintable waterproof "Ruberoid" roofing on the siding, ceiling, and floors. The interior exhibits appealed to contractors and skilled consumers alike with product lines of paints, varnishes, and insulating materials.

Hardware manufacturers also made the bridge between capital and consumer products. Large numbers of such exhibitors sold their goods "to the trade" while selling ordinary folks on the superiority of the merchandise. Presumably, they would ask local merchants to stock these goods thereby increasing sales. Enterprise Manufacturing Co. was one of many such multifaceted hardware vendors, along with Cattaraugus Cutlery Company and others. In their gleaming white and gold booth, the Philadelphia company appealed in part to the butcher and food processor with sausage makers, vinegar barrel taps, and the like. However, they also attracted the homeowner with time-savers such as lawn mowers and sprinklers. Modern homemakers were shown a range of items including "the family Coffee Mills, the Raisin Seeder, Cherry Pitter, Ice Shredder, and Food Chopper." Labor-saving devices, geared toward the more affluent middle-class, were becoming popular as servants became more costly and less available and as housework was becoming a greater burden to urban family operations.

John H. Patterson began manufacturing the cash register dubbed "the thief catcher" in 1884 and built an aggressive sales force to place it in retail outlets where it was intensely disliked by sales clerks. Distrustful store owners loved it for the records it kept of cash transactions, and National Cash Register soon dominated the market. NCR employees, however, were treated well, with extensive benefits from the company and many opportunities for self-improvement.

Underwood Typewriters was one of several manufacturers producing this practical office machine. Invented in 1876 in part to provide women with a clean, safe occupational alternative to mills and factories, it transformed the workforce from male scribes to female "Type Writers" by 1900. The typewriter's clarity appealed to others as well; it was adopted by Mark Twain who used it to write *Huckleberry Finn*.

Consumers were lured into the pavilions of
two nationally famous Boston chocolatiers,
Lowney's and Baker's. Lowney's offered
arrays of delectable chocolates, cocoas, and
bon-bons on the main level and exhibits of
products on the second floor. In the third
level roof garden, patrons could sit and
relax while enjoying their treats, then were
tempted to buy yet another small morsel
"for later" as they departed.

The Manufactures Building displayed modern consumer products. The urban household had
less time and less space for food preparation and storage. Heinz offered consumers tasty and
affordable condiments such as catsup and relishes to replace those once canned at home. Heinz
was the largest food exhibitor at the 1893 Chicago Columbian Exposition and was equally as
prominent in Buffalo.

Shredded Wheat was promoted as a health food. The Natural Food Company came to Niagara Falls in 1900 and there established a modern factory. Owner Henry Perky's philosophy of self-improvement and physical vitality spilled over into benevolent policies for employees who had numerous benefits and uplift programs supplied by the company. Western New York embraced several health crazes, and Shredded Wheat as a "restorative" became a popular cereal.

Health concerns made the "Hyde Portable Fountain" appealing. Manufactured in Rochester, these fountains eliminated the common cups used at other Pan-Am taps that were sources of contamination. The *New York Times* said how attractive was "this bending of the head above a sparkling little jet of water . . . to prevent the spread of contagious disease." The Hyde won a Silver Medal and was installed in the city's public schools.

Washburn-Crosby Company, predecessor to General Mills, was based in Minneapolis. Founded in Minnesota in 1889 as a partnership between two families, they pioneered all-roller-milling methods to produce the soft white flours used in pastries and light breads. In 1893, they had a growing national reputation for quality and wanted access to eastern markets. They thus opened a small warehouse on Fillmore at Clinton in Buffalo. Commercial milling was booming, fueled by demand from the bakery trades and from homemakers with no access to gristmills. The Queen City was an ideal site for expansion, located at the navigable end of the Great Lakes for grain shipping and near east coast markets where flour could be sold. The Pan-Am was merely prelude; by 1902, having outgrown the Fillmore Avenue location, they purchased the former Dakota Elevator site for their first Buffalo mill, then in 1903 Washburn-Crosby built a tile grain elevator on Buffalo's waterfront and launched a business that soon surpassed their Minneapolis operations.

Home sewing improved in 1846 when Elias Howe invented the sewing machine. Those unskilled in design, however, were left to rip apart one outfit to make up another. Paper patterns made by Butterick were a great success, and the patternmaker's booth was most popular. Inexpensive and reusable, patterns even provided home sewers with up-to-date fashions. Professional seamstresses also profited from using paper patterns rather than expensive muslin.

Most women's exhibits were dispersed throughout the Exposition; for example, Sophia Pratt's award-winning bookbinding was shown in Graphic Arts, and other businesses such as a rug outwork industry were displayed in Manufactures. The only concentrated presentation of "women's work" was in the Courtyard of the Liberal Arts Building where women shared the exhibit fees. Among the products on display and for sale were needlework, china and miniature painting, and weaving.

Agriculture was still important among the exhibits. The Horticulture Building featured everything from exotic Latin-American food plants one observer called "the best Pan-American exhibit of the Exposition," to commercial produce from 25 states. The Pan-Am created a sensation by refining the use of cold storage to preserve and display out-of-season produce. Another popular New York exhibit was devoted to Chautauqua grapes and wine making.

Another aspect of agriculture was important to the Americas; Superintendent F.A. Converse had a five-member committee overseeing the Apiarian exhibit on beekeeping and honey production, a critical aspect of farming worldwide. "Beekeeping as a pursuit may be regarded as one of no small importance." Over three hundred thousand beekeepers in the U.S. produced $200 million annually. The exhibit's superintendent was Orel L. Hershiser from Buffalo.

Examples of the nation's finest livestock were displayed in 15 barns just outside the Dairy Building on 10 acres of land near the East Amherst gate. Over two thousand animals were submitted for exhibit. From August through October, judges considered the merits of swine, cattle, sheep, horses, poultry, and even house pets. Daily demonstrations of milking and other dairy techniques attracted crowds of farmers and city folk alike.

The official catalogue listed the virtues of the Dairy Building. "In the center of the building is an exhibition case extending almost the entire length, carefully insulated, in order that its contents shall preserve that freshness which is always the charm of a well-kept dairy. Exhibits are arranged along the sides of the building and cooling plants are provided."

Arthur Goodrich wrote that "The United States Government Building is the most interesting on the grounds." It encompassed exhibits from virtually every federal department. Here A.W. Downing from the Philadelphia Mint operated a coin press that was fed blanks or "planchets" under 80 tons of pressure. It created souvenir medals, not money. The paper money press also printed souvenir pictures, including some of President McKinley after the September assassination.

The Coast and Geodetic Survey, under the direction of William Embeck, showed visitors various methods employed to obtain field data then to convert it into maps. The C&GS displayed examples of coastal maps for Boston and Charleston harbors; during the Expo they developed a contour map of the Niagara Frontier covering the river from Lake Erie to Lake Ontario and gave nearly two hundred thousand away during the course of the Exposition.

The Smithsonian Institution exhibits in the Government Building included selections from the National Museum's Department of Biology. Although officially touted as "of absorbing interest," there were only exceedingly formal presentations of stuffed birds, including a tiny case of hummingbirds, reptiles, mammals, and fish, all native to the Americas, including the United States and its newest possessions in the West Indies.

The exhibit from the Department of Geology had sought a skeleton of a mastodon, native to the Americas, to display, but none was found. Instead, a model of a triceratops was prepared for the Pan-Am, and it proved popular. The remaining installation included large cases occupied by "cave, hot-spring, and geyser deposits; concretions; and silicified woods." Still others were reserved for rocks from the recently annexed islands of Hawaii.

At 2:30 each afternoon the Lifesaving Service literally leapt into action. Crews first jumped into boats to rescue a "drowning man" in the lake. Then onshore crews fired a Lyel gun across the water to send ropes to a "marooned" vessel. The "imperiled" crews then slid to safety along the secured ropes in breeches buoys. Buffalo created a volunteer lifesaving service the following year.

Under the command of Capt. Edward L. Munson, the U.S. Hospital Corps demonstrated battlefield skills: carrying stretchers, lifting the wounded, first aid, and medical transport. The camp included 22 tents with a mess, a kitchen with a water purifier, a dispensary, and surgery. All gear could be stowed in "good sized trunks," including a stove capable of cooking for one hundred men. Three chests—medical, surgical, and sterilizer—comprised the entire hospital system.

With the Spanish-American War so recent, Exposition visitors were drawn to the Ordnance exhibits and demonstrations adjoining the U.S. Government building. Although the 1898 war had in no way involved a threat to the mainland, U.S. fears of invasion were a corollary to the nation's colonial and imperialist expansionism. One of the most popular demonstrations was offered by the 73rd Company, Coast Artillery. The 12-inch coastal defense gun was elevated for firing and lowered for loading. In operation the recoil would have assisted the lowering, but at the Pan-Am it was done with electricity. The October 25, 1900 Buffalo *Enquirer* reported excitedly that, "the disappearing carriage for this crowning feature of the ordnance exhibit is being built at Watertown, Mass., and the gun itself is now in the lathe at the federal arsenal at Watervliet." Exactly a year later, however, a reporter for the *Express* observed that ". . . Congress has now stopped the appropriation for disappearing guns, but there are enough on hand, I guess, anyhow."

Five

ON AND OFF THE MIDWAY

There was little doubt by summer 1901 that the Exposition was enormously popular. Although government and religious leaders forced "Sunday closings" that prohibited sales of anything except food, crowds continued to flock to the Fair for diversions and events as much as for exhibits. Virtually each day of the Exposition was designated for a show, spectacle, or sports. Dozens of nations, states, and professional and social organizations all had their "day" at the Expo: Vermont and Louisiana, Cuba and Mexico, Spanish-American veterans, nurses, the Knights of Columbus, and the Stationary Engineers were just a few of the groups honoring their own. The Midway, on the other hand, catered to all. Here were rides, novelties, amusements, and demonstrations of things unseen before. Curiously religious with its "Fall of Babylon" and "Jerusalem on the Day of Crucifixion" offerings, the Midway was also moderately salacious with "dancing girls," "giants," and "midgets." The Midway purported to educate while often extracting fees for merely mediocre presentations. Nevertheless, it remained a central destination for over 8.1 million visitors who came to see the spectacle.

Like the crowds shown arriving at Exchange Street station, young Ralph Burton and his parents were among the tourists flooding Buffalo needing accommodation. They had two beds at 573 Potomac for $2 per day. A *New York Times* reporter claimed some paid $4 for a cot and $5 for a "bed on a billiard table." Buffalo's $10 per week apartment dwellers were evicted to make way for visitors who paid $30 and $40 for their seven-day stay.

Railroads competed for tourists. The New York Central billed itself as THE line to the Exposition. To win riders, the Southern Pacific offered round trip fares and fees as low as 1¢ per mile. SPRR Pres. S.F.B. Morse said "nothing would be left undone . . . to augment attendance" at the Exposition, and SPRR joined forces with the *Los Angeles Times* to bring this "Pan-American Special" from California to Buffalo.

This crowd entering through the Lincoln Parkway gate on Decoration Day was typical. Although at first visitors were local, people came to Buffalo from across the continent. "The contrasts in the crowds is so marked that a host of individuals appear in a sea of faces," wrote one magazine reporter. However, there were few tourists from Latin-American nations, which were represented by a handful of dignitaries but very few visitors.

One of the Pan-American's most popular roving clowns, "The Yokel," caricatured the Exposition's crowds of visiting farmers from upstate towns such as Batavia, Clyde, Leroy, and Geneva. *New York Times* columnist William Drysdale mockingly observed that it seemed a waste of money to hire "The Yokel" to perform like a bumpkin, "making a great display of his greenness . . . when the real article was so plenty."

Music was "to be one of the greatest drawing cards of the Exposition." Popular musicians such as John Philip Sousa and Victor Herbert plus the Mexican Government Mounted Band and others performed in bandshells around the grounds. In addition, regular amateur presentations were offered where one could hear "good, indifferent, or distressing music according to the quality of the band which one happens to draw in the daily band lottery."

The Stadium offered free events to Exposition visitors, "a continuous carnival throughout the summer" according to the official program. It was the scene for major intercollegiate and international sports competitions, demonstrations such as the Firemen's Tournament, cattle and dairy shows, a week-long automobile show, and charity events for organizations such as the YMCA. Major holidays were celebrated by reviews of the troops and other patriotic displays.

Visitors created their own circuses. On "Railroad Day" in September, William McAlpine married Caro Clancy in a cage with four lions. The Reverend Charles Jones of Central Presbyterian Church officiated. It was a "hurried service" according to the newspaper. The stunt caught on. Lady Isola Hamilton, a model for "Around the World" on the Midway, picked the cage for her wedding to Harry Russell, the concessions' lecturer.

Midway Day drew attention to the "Lane of Laughter." The 1893 Chicago Columbian Exposition had the first Midway that was considered immoral. Buffalo Concessions Director Frederick W. Taylor boasted "The Pan" would be virtuous and would offer "much that is instructive and profitable." But Director of Amusement Louis Buckley revealed the important financial lure of the Midway as a permanent exposition fixture when he promised entertainment designed "to bring the crowds."

The Midway featured over 40 attractions including Thompson's Aerio-Cycle. A teeter-totter with revolving wheels at each end suspended often-terrified passengers 275 feet above the ground. Of the Midway's absurdities Richard Barry wrote, "The Midway—where everything that is amusing, grotesque, hilarious, foolish, novel, and absurd is foisted and intoned, where all that ingenuity can devise, skill project, or daring accomplish is brought for the diversions of a summer's day."

Even rain did not deter crowds. "The Midway is the most gigantic, the most complex, the most costly, and the most exciting plaything yet devised. . . . The longing for the whimsical return to boyishness and buncombe is one that lies deep seated in all natures." The Midway offered fun houses, rides, exotic settings, intelligent animals, and peculiar humans all eliciting both excitement and awe—all for 10¢ a show.

Buffalo residents DeWitt and Julia Greene of 1125 Main Street participated in one of the biggest attractions on the Midway, riding a camel on the "Streets of Cairo." Riding the camels became the "in" thing among socially prominent fairgoers. "A fad has seized the town," wrote one newspaper. The camels, it was claimed, were "trained down hard" to keep them docile and safe for even the most timid to ride.

A.Y. Pearson's Ostrich Farm found favor with young visitor Ralph Burton. There were 50 birds with several eggs in the 2 1/2-acre enclosure. Ralph learned the birds produced $100 worth of feathers each year. What impressed him more were their Victorian virtues. "The ostrich mates when about three years old," he wrote in his diary. "Once mated, they never mate again. As husband and wife they are sacredly true to each other."

Frank Bostock's Trained Wild Animals were a favorite. Bostock's grandfather, Sir Charles Wombwell, created the world's first zoo. Bostock's own menagerie was burned in January 1901 and hurriedly reassembled for the Pan-Am. In July, several animals broke loose causing pandemonium. In October, Jumbo the African elephant attacked and injured his keeper, Henry Mullen. Jumbo was to be publicly electrocuted in the Stadium for his deed, but public outcry spared his life.

The "Scenic Railway" miniature train entertained more adults than children. As part of a "railway and aquarama," it took passengers through electrically illuminated tunnels and through artificial landscapes. *New York Times* reporter William Drysdale, however, sneered particularly at "the ladies" who, he said, were so easily delighted by a trip in the tiny train past nothing but badly painted scenery.

The focal point of the Midway was the giant face of a sleeping woman beckoning visitors to J. F. Brown's "Dreamland." *National Magazine* wrote that this otherworldly image "suggests an Anglo-American Buddha." Visitors entered just under the head and inside encountered a maze of mirrors with images projected on their surfaces. One was of a young woman gently suspended in midair with her skirts billowing, demure yet alluring.

Alfred Swift introduced the Johnstown Flood exhibit at the Pan-Am. The 1889 Pennsylvania catastrophe still gripped public interest and "gave promise of financial reward" for the show. A "scenograph, the logical evolution of the cyclorama" presented the gathering storm, the bursting dam, torrents of floodwaters, and the hideous death of thousands. Nevertheless, Exposition officials and the public were assured it would be "more than an appeal to morbid taste."

The "Trip to the Moon" was one of the Exposition's few actual rides. Tourists entered the spaceship *Luna* where the craft began to vibrate and "we seemed . . . to see Buffalo and the Fair receding below us until we landed on the moon." The illusion was so good, reported a visitor, that an elderly woman became quite hysterical fearing she would never see home again.

At the Moon's Landing, "guides meet each excursion party on the Landing Dock and show them to the wonderful underground city of the moon, with its palaces and shops, and hordes of queer people." Along the passageway were "fungi, volcanic growths, stalactite drippings, crystallized mineral wonders . . ." Then "on to the marvelous palace of the 'Man in the Moon' where all are welcomed."

The City of the Moon "is an underground habitation of midgets and strange giants." The giants were over four times larger than the midgets. Enhancing routines offered by the performers contained many special effects. These were so well done that renowned inventor Thomas A. Edison praised the show's developer, Frederick Thompson for his innovative use of electricity.

Visitors were entertained. Wrote one tourist, "The Maids of the Moon gave us some songs and a skirt dance." One Maid was 12-year-old Hettie Kenton who performed her role over five thousand times during the Exposition. After the dance, however, "what somewhat spoiled the illusion was that when the show was over the door opened on one side and we were ushered directly from the moon to the streets of Buffalo."

Cuban-born Chiquita, "The Doll Lady of the Midway," was only 31 inches tall. Fluent in seven languages, she traveled the world receiving visitors in a tiny parlor. In November, Chiquita created her biggest sensation when she disappeared. It was soon revealed that she had eloped and was married. Her manager, F.C. Bostock, was more upset at the wedding than the disappearance for fear of losing so lucrative a performer.

Outsized "Maggie Murphy" was the "spieler" soliciting customers for "Dawson City: Land of the Midnight Sun." The attraction was a series of scenes, enhanced by electrical effects, leading visitors up the west coast to Alaska and featuring the January 1901 destruction of Dawson City by fire. A feud existed among this display, the Eskimo exhibit, and the Alaska Building with each claiming "the true story" of life in the frozen north.

The Schoellkopf family and others from Buffalo's German-American community replicated their heritage at "Alt Nurenberg." Nurenberg, Germany, a toy manufacturing center, had its medieval architecture faithfully reproduced including St. Sebald Church, the Gebhard astronomical clock, and the town hall complete with torture chambers. The attraction offered military bands, peasant theater, yodelers, and the town's famous "puppen" or dolls. The concession, funded by Buffalo capitalists, cost $60,000.

Crowds of visitors needed to be fed, and numerous restaurants and food concessions were scattered throughout the grounds. None was more elegant, however, than those at Alt Nurenberg. Buffalo brewer, Henry Fleishmann obtained rights to the Cafe Vienna that had graced the Paris World's Fair in 1900. More significantly, the exhibit attracted nationally renowned New York City restauranteur, August Luchow, whose German *haute cuisine* at the Pan-American was a great success.

One of the most peculiar Midway attractions was the Infant Incubator just east of the Service Building. The Qbata Company incubator was a marvel; it was an adaptation of those used to raise baby chicks, with controlled heat and ventilation offering life support to newborns who otherwise would have died. For only 10¢ the curious could file past the "couveuse," as the incubator was called at the Paris Exposition, and marvel at this scientific advance. *Cosmopolitan* magazine said of the display, "These tiny babies prematurely born lie on miniature beds in neat little ovens from which they are taken at regular intervals to be fed, weighed, and reswathed." During the Exposition, premature triplets were rushed to Buffalo from New York City and along with twins and several babies from the Indian Congress were kept in incubators until they were strong enough to thrive. They did so well that actress Sarah Bernhardt remarked during her visit that the stork on Alt Nurenberg should have been on the Incubator Building. After the Exposition, some of the equipment was installed at Children's Hospital.

C.D. Arnold of Bidwell Parkway became the Exposition's official photographer. He was paid for his documentary photographs but was to construct his own studio, shown here, and pay a concession fee for any photographs he sold. In return, the director of Works erected two 40-foot towers for Arnold's panoramic shots. He also had a booth in the Ethnology Building, but it was initially set behind a door and was useless.

Because Arnold had exclusive rights to sell Exposition photographs, controls on private cameras were tight. All cameras required a permit at 50¢ daily, none could have photograph plates larger than 4 x 5 inches, and none could have tripods. Camera smuggling became common, with perpetrators hiding their equipment in lunchboxes, handbags, and the like. "Camera police" looked for the daily passes, without which cameras were fined, confiscated, or both.

Managing the Exposition involved law enforcement. Director of Works Newcomb Carlton vowed to create a professional police outfit. He told the *Buffalo Express* that "there will be no flummery uniforms and no tin toadstabbers in the equipment of the Exposition guards, but they will wear the plain blue clothes and carry the same plain locust club that the masses of American people have been taught to fear, if not to respect." During construction there were only 50 officers, but after Opening Day, the force, comprised largely of returned Spanish-American War veterans, tripled. The Board of Directors applied to the city council for a bond of $150,000 to support the department, but the request was denied. Only the military steadfastly opposed a police presence, insisting the army should guard government exhibits. In general, officers faced minimal and largely non-violent crime until the final day when theft and fighting over goods was rampant. *New York Times* columnist William Drysdale wrote that if they arrested those taking money on false pretenses, they should have looked to Midway shopkeepers first.

No great exposition would have been complete without a Bazaar. It housed the telegraph, express office, post office, and newspaper headquarters for both the public and concessionaires. It also, as its name implies, sold the official souvenirs, keepsakes, and trinkets so desired by visitors along with a variety of goods for which the exhibits had no room. Everything from toys to player pianos was there.

Concessions were the financial lifeblood of the Exposition. The directors contracted everything from the large exhibits to chocolate bon-bons and peanuts (no shells). In Chicago, Omaha, and Nashville the expositions all had roller chairs shown here with Pan-American Police Commandant Col. John Byrne. Chairs rented by the hour or day and were highly lucrative. One official punned, "the man who gets the roller-chair concession will be decidedly in the push." John Dagget won the valued contract.

Getting around the Pan-American was accomplished easily via the canal system. Gondolas were part of the "Venice in America" display on the Midway and were available for hire to tour the Exposition at a leisurely pace. There were landings at various strategic points where one could disembark, tour an exhibit, then return for another languorous journey to the next destination.

Abergo & Baroni's electric launches were the favored form of transport for those desiring to circumnavigate the perimeter of the Pan-American in an expeditious manner. Inventor Thomas A. Edison employed one of the launches to photograph virtually every inch of the canal system and its adjoining built environment. Edison shot hundreds of photographs from which a detailed record of the canal journey can still be recreated.

Six

CAPTIVE HERITAGE

There were two May 20, 1901 Dedication Day parades for the Pan-American Exposition; the concessionaires' gala set the tone for the Exposition's treatment of other cultures. The Pan-American theme of human progress from "savage" to "civilized" reinforced negative attitudes toward people of color. These perceptions were also related to the modernist notions that drove the Exposition: everything western and industrial was good; all else was inferior, suffering at best from what early anthropology dubbed a "cultural lag." The foreign-village type of Midway show was introduced at the 1889 Paris Fair and expanded at Chicago in 1893. In Buffalo, directors made a clear if unwarranted distinction between "scholarly" explorations of culture in the Exposition buildings and popular "ethnologies" on the Midway where people from different cultures became living exhibits. Director-General Buchanan made the distinction economic. He disdained the Ethnology exhibits because there was no commercial payback. He wrote, "it would certainly have been better to have omitted that division from the classification and building plans. Certainly the result was far from satisfactory."

Formal ethnology, the study of human cultures, was presented in the Government and Ethnology buildings. In the former, the Smithsonian Institution's National Museum contributed elaborate dioramas of 12 native family groupings from the Americas such as the Navaho weavers shown here. Each model was based on a small number of families investigated by anthropologists. The displays thus reflected both the knowledge and misunderstandings inherent in generalizing from limited experiences.

While the Smithsonian depicted scenes of life and work such as the Sioux diorama, Ethnology Building Director A.L. Benedict offered only cultural maps and artifacts. He despaired of producing anything of interest since he believed "Large portions of North America yield aboriginal relics . . . indicating no very distinct differences of culture." His poorly interpreted artifacts came chiefly from hobby collections of friends and colleagues, not from Native Americans themselves.

Ethnology displays included the 3,000-year-old mummy of a Chilean woman shipped to the Exposition from Santiago. Spanish prejudice against Native Americans was voiced by Chilean Julio Perez Canto who wrote to Benedict that there were few relics from South America "that would demonstrate the lives of the savage tribes that inhabited our territory as they were very uncivilized, and when they disappeared they left no trace of their existence."

Seneca carpenters built log cabins supposedly reproducing four hundred years of housing among the Six Nations at the Do-she-wea Yo-cen-ger-dad or Buffalo Village. Mohawks were to live on site and purvey native customs and work for passersby. This cabin was the home of 106-year-old Nancy Johnson. She, her daughter Jane Doxtater, and the cabin were relocated from the Tonawanda Reservation. Nancy was to live there "and receive and entertain her friends in her own Indian way."

October 20, 1900.

Anthropology was also on the Midway. "Whatever there is of ethnological value on the . . . Midway is there for other than scientific reasons . . . for though students go to the Midway, they do not go for study." Buffalo boasted of the Midway's morality, but the lure was in seeing people, depicted as less than human, in various stages of nudity giving titillating performances otherwise unacceptable in late Victorian society.

Akoun's Beautiful Orient promised all the allure of life on the Streets of Cairo. The fulfillment of actual customs cost Gaston Akoun dearly. Contractually obligated to provide holy water for Muslim holidays, he forgot, then quietly substituted expensive Apollinaire bottled water instead. Rather than using it to bless kegs of tap water, the residents liked it, drank it, and Akoun had to keep supplying this expensive version or have his duplicity revealed.

Efforts to depict "real" life in the compounds did find people practicing crafts and production such as these young rug weavers. The Fair's directors were oblivious to social issues such as child labor since it was equally a part of U.S. industrial production as well. Discussions of child health and welfare were remanded to the Liberal Arts Building and conveniently divorced from Midway settings where hazards actually existed.

Only the Japanese were welcomed to the Exposition as near equals. As a burgeoning imperialist power, victors of the 1895 Sino-Japanese war, they had adopted many western institutions. Their exhibit was still predominantly a sideshow featuring not only reproductions of the Emperor's residence and Nikkei Temple but also dancers, jugglers, acrobats, and geisha girls. However, their jinrikishas were licensed to provide transport on an equal basis with "western" concessions.

The Philippines, a colonial trophy from the Spanish-American War, occupied a large part of the Exposition. The 11-acre compound, based on the village of Binondo, had one hundred residents living on site with a cookhouse, dining room, huts, and quarters for unmarried residents. Livestock including chickens and 12 water buffalos roamed the enclosure. The village was guarded by U.S. soldiers "to lend the necessary military aspect to the scene."

The Filipino's manager, "Pony" Moore, promised "representatives of all the races inhabiting the islands, ranging from cannibalism to the highest degree of civilization." Some hoped that divisions among Filipinos would incite conflict but little occurred. Performers included bolo sword fighters, but ordinary people such as Brawleo Barbaya, a taxidermist and his family, impressed crowds with their dignity and grace as he and others practiced their crafts and customs.

The display on Inuits, known at the Pan-Am as the "Esquimaux," was championed by Pres. William McKinley. The exhibit was first offered by Mr. Wanta Cinchee whose ice company offered to make eternal winter possible in Buffalo. It was not an enticement. The exhibit finally occurred and assembled representatives of three groups from the Hudson Straits to demonstrate seal hunting, fishing, and other aspects of daily lives.

Visitor Ralph Burton wrote, "In this village it was all arranged as at home, with their huts, dogs, etc. They gave us an athletic exhibition on a stage." Alaskans demonstrated dog sleds and how they used bear and seal skins. They erected a hut made entirely of whalebone, one of a kind, which was coveted by the French Anthropological Society but was given to the Smithsonian Institution.

Despite the harmless child spieler outside, African Village inhabitants were portrayed as fascinating but dangerous: "African warriors from Darkest Africa—Assegal Throwers, Zulus, Cannibals . . ." Sixty-two people supposedly representing 35 tribes were brought to Buffalo to demonstrate weapons, handicrafts, songs, dances, and it was said, witchcraft. Only one, John Tivie, had been outside Africa before, to Chicago in 1893, and they all remained secluded in their compound.

African Village organizer was Frenchman Xavier Pene, who recruited a wide range of people to participate. He told westerners wild tales of his encounters with poison-dart-throwing pygmies and his brush with death at their hands. The Africans did in fact perform traditional dances, some of extraordinary daring, but they were largely skilled craftspeople who practiced their daily routines of carving, weaving, basketry, and smithing as well as household duties.

The two young women, Mary Acrobessie and Mucay Oku, were members of the village society. Mary's father was a goldsmith who practiced his skill for the Pan-American crowds. The degree of ability and knowledge present within the compound was ignored by some visitors who wanted only to see the Africans practice vile and unspeakable acts despite the fact that those were largely fictions created by the promoters.

Carlos E. Cummings of the Buffalo Society of Natural Sciences claimed great familiarity with the anthropology of African life. He spent virtually every day at the compound "in the interest of the Society." After the Exposition, Cummings touted his expertise in lectures where he offered to describe the arts and crafts, native trades, and "the innumerable comical and pathetic phases of the African performances while here."

103

Little thought was given to the plight of Africans come autumn. Used to equatorial conditions, they were given no provisions for warmth. They had small cooking stoves that were insufficient for heating living spaces. They were finally given complicated gas stoves that were not explained. Instead the Africans were simply forbidden to light them without a "white attaché" present. When no one came September 26, their own attempts to light the unfamiliar stove caused an explosion that injured one man. Simply to stay warm the Africans assembled whatever cast-off American clothes they could acquire, leading newspapers to deride them saying they "present a most ludicrous appearance." At the end of the Exposition, hardships worsened. In late October the infant son of Tomasso Quayeo died. He was taken to the hospital in an ambulance but was simply left in the vehicle. When cleaning crews found the tiny body, they threw it in the trash. When it was discovered, the coroner finally arrived and the child's body was properly tended. The family, however, left Buffalo unconsoled.

E.S. Dundy's "Old Plantation" was made acceptable by changing national circumstances. In 1895, Booker T. Washington installed an exhibit on Negro Education in the South at the Atlanta Cotton States Centennial Exposition. The 1896 Supreme Court decision, *Plessy v. Ferguson*, validated "Jim Crow" segregation laws in southern states giving license nationally to a resurgence of racial discrimination. The "Old Plantation" freely portrayed Black American life with bigotry and disrespect.

"Laughing Ben" was the Plantation's image of "good negroes," the "Uncles and Aunties" who were genial and compliant. By contrast, Buffalo's African-American community had met at Michigan Street Baptist Church to promote a Negro Exhibit such as Atlanta's. The movement was led by Mrs. John Dover, vice president of the Phyllis Club of Colored Women, politician James Ross, and educator Mary Talbert who was recommended as commissioner for the exhibit.

The Plantation offered the stereotypical image of "Three Cullud Gemmen." Earlier, however, W.E.B. DuBois had created a full-scale exhibit on African-American achievement, an official U.S. entry at the 1900 Paris World's Fair. Commissioner Thomas Calloway came to Buffalo in December 1900 to propose using that exhibit at the Pan-American, and Congress approved $15,000 for the installation. It depicted Black achievements in education, industrial work, literature, journalism, and more.

The Plantation showed a cabin from Jefferson Davis's estate as a "typical" African-American home. By contrast the Paris exhibit "showing the development of the Negro race since . . . the Emancipation Proclamation" was installed in the Social Economy section of the Liberal Arts Building. It included photodocumentation on educational institutions such as Tuskegee, Fisk, and Howard University. Unfortunately, this presentation on African-American achievements could not offset the spectacles on the Midway.

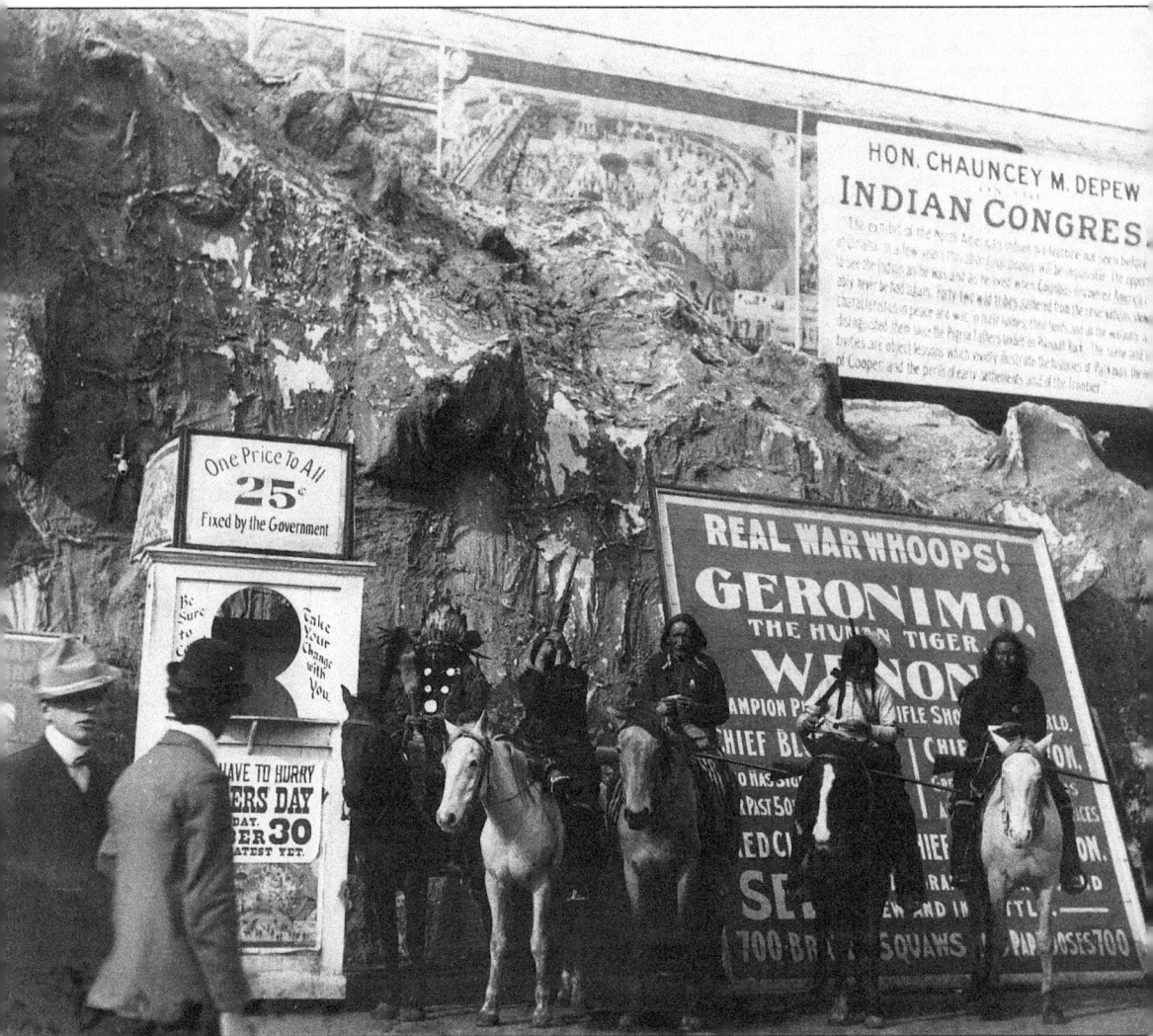

The closing of America's frontier in the 1890s spelled the end of independence for Native-American nations. The incessant move westward and settlement of land first by railroads then by farmers and ranchers had pushed indigenous people from their age-old territories onto reservations. Many who fought the relentless incursions into their homelands were captured and imprisoned by the U.S. government. As tribes and nations were "pacified," ambitious promoters such as Frederick T. Cummins saw the new economic dependency of native peoples as an opportunity to direct them into show business. He went on an "Indian Hunt" to find five hundred "braves and squaws" from 42 different tribes to portray "authentic" Native-American life in the "greatest aggregation of living American Indians ever presented to the public." The *Pan-American Magazine* urged the display. "Without Native Americans a Pan-American exhibition would be like an old time circus without the clown." When the show in Buffalo was over, the hapless families packed up and headed to another round of living on display on lands far from home.

Cummins, shown with Chief White Hawk, Hand Bear, and Chief Black Bear, established the 1898 Omaha Congress with 34 tribes. His partner, George Gaines, was an army official at the Battle of Wounded Knee. They supposedly "understood" Native Americans and "bravely" united mortal enemies, but they included the Six Nations who had never even encountered Plains dwellers much less fought them. Also Cummins erected only tepees for housing thus invalidating claims of cultural accuracy.

The highlight of the Congress was the daily "sham battle." They were touted as "battles between the different tribes which at times will border more on the realistic than the sham, war dances, sun dances, and dances of different feasts and to their various Gods, in which the braves will appear in all the glory of war paint and feathers." One Buffalo reporter estimated that 15,000 rounds of blank ammunition were expended each performance.

Hock See Ocka, a Winnebago girl, was a dancer. At her young age she was charged with conveying something of her culture to paying customers. The performances, like many other aspects of life in the Congress, tended to blend into homogeneous presentations as cultural differences yielded to efficient showmanship. Individualized crafts such as beadwork and moccasins survived only because they were made for sale by individual women of the Congress.

Promoters bragged that women and children could visit the village alone, and they "will have protection and instruction." White women interested in social reform flocked to the Congress to examine living conditions, clearly with no qualms about invading privacy. *New York Times* reporter William Drysdale said the modern woman visitor was too serious. "If there are 42 tribes . . . she feels a duty to see every one of them."

Adolescent diarist Ralph Burton wrote, "There were many Indians in their tent homes, with their babies and domestic utensils. The sham battle was fine as well as their war dances and other dances. The old warrior chief, Geronimo, a U.S. prisoner, was there and took part in the exercises. We had a near view of him and other noted Chiefs. He is said to be 88 years old." Geronimo, whose real name was Goyathlay, was promoted as a killer and a savage. An Apache, he had traveled to several earlier expositions also escorted under armed guard as a federal prisoner. His old age was at best ignominious. For a promotion in August, Exposition handlers took him to H.A. Meldrum Co. department store as a display. In September, newspapers announced that he would demonstrate to "squaws" how to do white man's cooking. The papers also reported that after the assassination of Pres. William McKinley, Geronimo openly mourned the president's death. At the conclusion of the Pan-Am, Geronimo's supporters tried to obtain his freedom, but he was not released. He died in 1909.

Seven

ASSASSINATION
AND AFTERMATH

Buffalo eagerly awaited September 5–6 when President and Mrs. William McKinley would visit the Exposition. He would present two speeches, and they would both attend numerous celebrations such as the review of troops shown here. The President was an avid supporter of American capital and military expansion. However, at a time when fewer than ten percent of the New York City population was middle class, working people struggled for bare survival. The ongoing Great Merger Movement threatened small business as unfettered corporate acquisitions either absorbed competitors or ruined them. At the edge of these conflicts was anarchist Leon Czolgosz who saw no alternative but to destroy the system and McKinley. Following the President's assassination, the Exposition continued but was burdened by its own problems. The concluding days were characterized by organizational chaos and financial disgrace. The Pan-American Exposition unintentionally became Buffalo's swan song. Those who underwrote both the city and the event gradually began to drift away to other places and ventures, leaving only a glistening memory of a golden moment.

On September 5, President McKinley made his first appearance at the Pan-American. Although scheduled to attend earlier in June, his wife's fragile health had forced him to halt a trip through the west and to cancel his Buffalo plans. His September presentation drew huge crowds of visitors and reporters alike. The latter are arrayed along the front of the platform recording McKinley's declaration that "Expositions are the timekeepers of progress."

President and Mrs. McKinley arrive at the Exposition the morning of September 6, 1901. Due to the press of time, they were scheduled to go their separate ways to fulfill the numerous obligations before them. McKinley was headed to Niagara Falls, and Mrs. McKinley would remain in Buffalo. This was the last time they would be happily together before events conspired to keep them apart forever.

112

McKinley and Pan-Am President Milburn arrived on the Exposition grounds having returned from a trip to Niagara Falls where they spent the morning with other officials including Dr. Roswell Park who remained behind. During his stay in Buffalo, the President was driven by coachman William McGee who handled two French coaching horses, Cogent and Crescent. They would, ironically, remain the President's means of transport through his funeral.

McKinley was served lunch at the Mission Building, which, despite its name, housed a number of Buffalo business exhibits. McKinley was guest of the Birge wallpaper company, which had a display at the site. Mrs. McKinley, a longtime sufferer from epilepsy, had been feted at the Women's Building and was to stay for lunch, but during the reception she grew ill and had to withdraw from all further events.

LESLIE'S WEEKLY ILLUSTRATED

Vol. XCIII—No. 2402

New York, September 21, 1901

PRICE 10 CENTS

THE FOULEST CRIME OF THE NEW CENTURY

AN ANARCHIST'S ATTEMPT, AT THE BUFFALO EXPOSITION, TO MURDER THE MOST POPULAR OF OUR AMERICAN PRESIDENTS—DRAWN BY T. DART WALKER, OUR SPECIAL ARTIST AT THE PAN-AMERICAN EXPOSITION.

McKinley arrived at the Temple of Music to address the crowd. An unnamed eyewitness described Leon Czolgosz's assault on McKinley at 4:30 p.m. "I felt the pulse of a nation quicken and throb in glad response to the proud honor of the occasion. . . . Suddenly two shots in quick succession rang out from the building within. Instantly a hush fell upon the multitude far and near. . . . A whisper began to pass from mouth to mouth like an electric current, 'The President has been shot!' Low murmurs on the part of the men and quiet sobbing from the women began to slacken the tension. Suddenly the clanging bell of an ambulance was heard. . . . All at once some one caught sight of a man being conducted to a carriage, and the cry broke out, 'The assassin!' . . . Cries of 'Lynch him!' 'Shoot him!' 'Kill the brute!' rent the air about me, and made me shudder at the sudden awakening of vindictive and vengeful desire. . . . The exhibition of these contrasting elements in human nature in so brief a space of time is indelibly fixed in my memory."

114

Czolgosz, a 25-year-old American-born blacksmith's helper from Cleveland, said he became an anarchist in 1895. He arrived in Buffalo the Saturday prior to McKinley's speech and boarded at Albert Nowak's, 1025 Broadway, as "John Doe." When he was shown his room by law clerk James Walkowiak, he claimed he was Fred Niemin. His confession was recorded but never publicly released "to prevent his becoming a hero."

James Benjamin Parker did become a hero. A waiter at the Exposition's Plaza Restaurant, he stood just ahead of Czolgosz who jostled him, possibly readying the gun. Parker let Czolgosz proceed, then, when Czolgosz shot McKinley, Parker "grabbed and throttled him," preventing a third shot and holding him for arrest. Parker, an African American, received scant official recognition for his deed, but the public loved him. Customers tried to sit at his tables and left large tips and notes of admiration.

McKinley was rushed by ambulance to the Exposition's Emergency Hospital rather than being transported to Buffalo General Hospital. With Dr. Roswell Park still out of town, McKinley waited in great pain for over an hour. Board President Milburn recommended Dr. M.D. Mann as surgeon even though Mann had no experience with gunshot wounds. Other physicians at the scene were Drs. P.M. Rixey, Herman Mynter, Eugene Wasdin, and E.W. Lee.

Roswell Park

Roswell Park was a leader in Buffalo medicine, especially in antiseptic practice. Dr. Mann and the others were neither trained trauma surgeons nor did they bother with disinfection, not even wearing gloves. The first bullet had done little harm; the second entered McKinley's abdomen. The physicians used improperly sanitized probes, and when Mann could not find the bullet, he closed the incision without draining the wound. It was a fateful decision.

At 7:30 p.m., McKinley was moved from the Pan-Am Hospital to Milburn's home at 1168 Delaware Avenue. Crowds quickly assembled, and the entire Delaware area from Linwood to Tudor along West Ferry and Cleveland was roped off to keep curiosity seekers and sympathizers at bay. Guards from Ft. Porter were deployed to maintain absolute quiet, and all vehicles were stopped and kept from the area.

Tents were erected just outside the rope barriers to provide informal offices for the press. Other journalists worked from the nearby home of Mrs. Harriet Mack, a member of the Board of Women Managers. Even the telegraph operator, originally placed in the Milburns's carriage house, was relocated due to noise.

Mrs. McKinley stayed near her husband, but other than family only top-level government officials saw the stricken President. Buffalo virtually became the seat of government while the world waited for word of the President's condition. Vice Pres. Theodore Roosevelt and Sen. Mark Hanna, the new face and the old guard of the Republican Party, were two of the rare few admitted to the Milburn house.

The Buffalo Club on Delaware Avenue near Tupper functioned as the Cabinet offices, and most of the cabinet secretaries and Vice President Roosevelt lived at this site. State Secretary Hay and Naval Secretary Long were absent, and Secretary of War Elihu Root stayed with Buffalo business leader Howard Sprague, a close relative. Western Union immediately strung telegraph wires into the club so the hub of government could continue to function.

Since the bullet had not been recovered and the stomach wounds were sewn shut, the physicians watched the President's condition with concern. Thomas Edison rushed a portable X-ray machine to Buffalo to assist the doctors if a second surgical foray for the bullet became necessary. Other equipment was provided for McKinley's comfort. Charles Huntley, founder of Buffalo General Electric, sent electric fans and special wiring.

The physicians shown here announced McKinley's vital signs daily saying he was recovering. He did improve until the doctors decided he should eat solid food that overtaxed his badly infected system. Dr. Charles Stockton ordered heart stimulants, and on September 13, McKinley received digitalis and strychnine; he rallied only to bid his wife good-bye. He died at 2:15 a.m. September 14, victim of the medical system as much as the assassin's bullet.

Buffalo, Washington, and the nation were stunned by the President's death. Services were planned at numerous locations in Buffalo, the capital, and Canton, Ohio, where McKinley was to be buried. At 10 a.m. Sunday, September 15, a small funeral was held in the Milburn home with only the family, Cabinet secretaries, and a handful of friends present. Delaware Avenue remained roped off as the casket was removed, and the crowds kept a respectful silence.

Around noon the funeral procession was assembled for the long march to city hall on Franklin Street where McKinley's remains were to lie in state. The honor guard consisted of men from all service branches including the New York National Guard. Harper's Weekly wrote "The streets were thronged with reverential crowds, who bared their heads and freely let the tears course down their cheeks as the cortege passed on."

120

From 1:30 to 11 p.m. Sunday, McKinley lay in state in city hall (now county hall). It was estimated that over one hundred thousand people passed by the open casket, and still more waited patiently on the streets around Franklin and Church. The doors were closed at ten minutes before 11 p.m., leaving hundreds of people outside. Both Saturday and Sunday all illumination, exhibits, and amusements at the Exposition were canceled. Concessionaires were not happy. The President's death had vastly improved their sales of trinkets bearing the image of McKinley and his wife. There had been a conflict earlier in the week when some exhibitors voluntarily closed in respect for the ailing president and others; the largest did not. *Harper's Weekly* reported that during the Sunday public mourning, among those showing the greatest concern was a 50-member delegation from the Indian Congress that came to the viewing. Geronimo purportedly created a lament, and the delegation to city hall came bearing a wreath of asters inscribed 'To the Great White Chief.'

Monday morning the casket left Buffalo. The seven-car train carrying McKinley's remains had been used by the President in June, and his family was attended by the same Pullman conductor, W.M. Johnson. McKinley's casket was alone in the elegant observation car, the "Pacific." The coffin rested on a catafalque draped with the American flag, carrying a wreath and crossed swords for its final journey to the nation's capital.

Vice Pres. Theodore R. Roosevelt rushed back to Buffalo the afternoon following McKinley's death. After paying his respects to the widow, he proceeded to the Delaware Avenue home of Ansley Wilcox. At 3:30 p.m., wearing a borrowed cutaway coat and striped trousers, Roosevelt was sworn into the Presidency by Judge John R. Hazel. There were no pictures since an interloper had deliberately damaged the authorized camera, and Roosevelt barred any other photographs.

Czolgosz was tried immediately. Eleven of the jurors and Deputy Sheriffs Charles Brady and Albert Haskel are pictured here. Defended by a court-appointed law firm, Czolgosz remained silent. The jury retired at 3:51 p.m. September 23, and returned their guilty verdict at 4:26 p.m. Czolgosz was sentenced to death and was electrocuted October 29. Anti-radical reprisals were swift; even Czolgosz's father was fired and evicted from his home.

The Temple of Music became the object of morbid curiosity and a shrine. The spot where McKinley had stood "was marked within 15 minutes of the shooting by James L. Quackenbush who was present." Guards were posted, and a railing was built around the site to prevent splinters of the platform being taken. A visitor from Massillion, Ohio, noticed that the grain of the wood inside the rail resembled McKinley's profile, and crowds surged in to see the image.

The Pan-American Board of Directors had barely recovered from McKinley's death when its own problems surfaced. The board had sold stocks and bonds on the premise that "the demand for concessions is an assurance of the success of the Exposition." However, their elaborate plans based on a desire to outshine other expositions, cost more than estimated, and expenses outstripped revenues two-to-one. By October 22, it was clear that only the original mortgage holders would receive any money. Contractors, however, secured mechanics' liens, and in November, they sent the sheriff to confiscate Exposition deposits. Accountant Henry Nicholls discovered the plan, and he and Treasurer George Williams smuggled $50,000 into a waiting ambulance. They drove the vehicle past the sheriff to Williams's house shown here at Delaware and North. There they secreted the money in Williams's basement vault. It was deposited the next day at Guaranty Trust on behalf of the first mortgage bond holders. No other claims were ever fully satisfied, and contractors lost over $1 million for their work.

The final days of the Exposition were melancholy. Buffalo mourned the loss of international prominence; Exposition visitors worried about clearance sales of merchandise; employees worried about survival. Hundreds of widows with children had been gainfully employed but now faced public relief. The directors and concessionaires staged elaborate farewell banquets. As Buffalo's dignitaries congregated the last day, Mrs. Harriet Mack wrote in her memoir, "On November 2nd the closing ceremonies were held in the Temple of Music. Taps sounded. John Milburn touched the button, the lights of the Electric Tower faded out to the strain 'Nearer My God To Thee.' There were tears in every eye. Something very beautiful was lost to us forever." Concessions moved on, many to Charleston, South Carolina, scene of the 1902 Exposition. Director of Works Carlton began preparing inventories of every scrap of roofing, lumber, and plumbing to reduce the cost of demolition. *Harper's Weekly* wrote that despite the beauty and distinction, the financial burden of the Exposition might make Buffalo look back on the show the way Chicago and Boston looked back on their great fires.

No one wished to relinquish the glory. Immediately after closing, proposals to retain something of the 'Rainbow City' began to circulate. Groups tried to protect and reinforce the Electric Tower; others suggested the site might be the newest National Park. The New York State Building did become the Historical Society; J.N. Adam donated the Aeolian Organ from the Temple of Music to Elmwood Music Hall, and many of the fine arts pieces went to the new Albright Gallery. But the board had contracted to restore the Rumsey Farm exactly as before, with canals filled, pilings removed, and all structures destroyed. Demolition was awarded to Chicago House Wrecking, and by March 1902 the Exposition was in ruins. The *Courier* wrote, "Everywhere are strewn broken columns, disfigured reliefs and mutilated statues. Some of these are really grotesque. . . . The gardens are strewn with broken lamp posts, leafless tree branches, and pieces of broken sculpture. The winding waterways are a mass of melting ice, of mud and of plaster." On a brighter note, Congress provided the much-needed financial bailout, and bankruptcy was averted.

The image of fickle children choosing playmates understated Buffalo's transitions. From its 1899 inception, the Lackawanna Steel Plant was compared to the Pan-Am. Even the ornate Beaux-Arts office building was supposedly an echo of the Exposition, and wood from the Midway built homes for plant workers. But the mill was just one of the changes in Buffalo's economy, not all of them good. Lackawanna Iron & Steel was controlled by Wall Street. By 1920, it was in ruins before being acquired by another absentee owner, Bethlehem Corporation. More important, some of Buffalo's leaders such as Milburn and Williams left the city immediately after the Pan-Am. Others gradually shifted their capital away from local business. Buffalo succeeded well in using the Pan-American to attract national interests but slowly lost control over its own destiny to those outsiders. Despite these problems, the *Courier* wrote the proper epitaph. "You miss the Exposition—if you're a Buffalonian. You'll never again have so much entertainment laid down at your doors. . . . You have got a heap of enjoyment out of it, and you have not 'gone broke' either."

ACKNOWLEDGMENTS

This book could not have been written without the kind cooperation of the Buffalo & Erie County Historical Society. Thanks are due to Exec. Dir. William Siener who opened the Society's extensive Pan-American Exposition photographic collections for this collaboration. Further thanks go to the excellent library staff members including BECHS Library and Archives Dir. Mary Bell, Assoc. Librarian Pat Virgil, Asst. Librarian Cathy Mason, and Library Asst. Yvonne Foote. Interpretation Coordinator Virginia Bartos shared much of her extensive research particularly relating to the Board of Women Managers. We also appreciate the unfailing support of Roberta Carmina and Elaine Schmidt who helped to keep us organized and on track.

We are grateful to the staff of Special Collections at the Buffalo & Erie County Public Library whose Pan-American collections proved invaluable. William Loos, Curator of the Rare Book Room and his assistant, Andrew Maines were most cooperative especially in securing the reproduction of C.D. Arnold's studio and other photographic duplications. We also relied on the work of the very knowledgeable and helpful staff in the library's Local History Section, Robert Gurn, Cynthia Van Ness, and Patricia Monahan. Doris Ursitti at the Theodore Roosevelt Inaugural National Historic Site helped with inauguration information.

Several of the heavy industry photographs in Chapter Four on Exhibits (p.62B, 63, 64B, and 65) came from the wonderful journal, *Iron Age* (now *New Steel*) owned by Chilton Publishing who generously permitted their reproduction. In Washington, D.C. Helena Wright and Rhoda Rattener clarified issues surrounding the reproduction of Pan-American photographs from the Smithsonian's 1901 annual report.

Thanks are due to many contemporary photographers: Paul Maze of Phototech, Steve Mangione, and John Jackson at Delaware Camera & Video. Our good friend, Lauren Belfer, shared references from her own work. We also appreciated the comments of Martin Wachadlu whose knowledge of architectural history was most useful. Our most profound debt is to the late and deeply missed architectural historian, Austin Fox whose love of Buffalo and the Pan-Am set much of this in motion.

Finally, we thank our colleagues at Arcadia Press for all of their assistance, especially Rebecca Heflin and Sarah Maineri who shepherded this volume through the publishing maze.

www.ingramcontent.com/pod-product-compliance
Lightning Source LLC
Chambersburg PA
CBHW050923150426
42812CB00051B/1991

* 9 7 8 1 5 3 1 6 3 7 1 4 9 *